GUITAR WORLD PRESENTS

NIRVANA and the GRUNGE REVOLUTION

THE SEATTLE SOUND
The story of how Kurt Cobain
and his Seattle cohorts changed
the face of rock in the Nineties.
Featuring interviews with
Alice In Chains, Soundgarden,
Pearl Jam and other grunge stars.

From the pages of
GUITAR WORLD
magazine

Edited by
**Jeff Kitts, Brad Tolinski
and Harold Steinblatt**

Published by Hal Leonard Corporation
In cooperation with Harris Publications, Inc. and Guitar World Magazine
Guitar World is a registered trademark of Harris Publications, Inc.

7777 W. BLUEMOUND RD. P.O. BOX 13819 MILWAUKEE, WI 53213

ISBN 0-7935-9006-X
Copyright © 1998 by HAL LEONARD CORPORATION
International Copyright Secured   All Rights Reserved

Executive Producer: Brad Tolinski
Producer: Carol Flannery
Editors: Jeff Kitts & Harold Steinblatt
Art Director: John Flannery
Cover photo and editorial photos: Charles Peterson

Visit Hal Leonard Online at
www.halleonard.com

Table of Contents

FEATURES

SOUNDGARDEN

Seattle Reign

The Rise and Fall of Seattle Grunge.

By Jon Wiederhorn

I

T'S ONE OF the most instantly recognizable videos from the Nineties: In a smoke-filled basketball gym, tattooed cheerleaders with anarchy symbols on their jet-black uniforms twirl their pompoms, while a dirty blonde guitarist with unwashed hair and a striped sweater strums vociferously at his black and white Stratocaster. Even without the scenes of the crowd moshing hysterically, a janitor swaying back and forth, or even shots of the other two band members, everyone with cable TV should be able to identify the clip as Nirvana's "Smells Like Teen Spirit."

By January 1992, the video was being played constantly on MTV, and the song could be heard everywhere—on radio, in record stores, even from buskers on street corners. Within days, Nirvana would replace Michael Jackson for the top slot on the *Billboard* album chart. A new era had dawned, and teen spirit was running rampant. Grunge had been transformed from a small regional scene to a global phenomenon, and the entire music industry was about to mutate into a beast that would turn its back on slickly produced pop and glam metal in favor of ragged, swampy noise that emphasized emotional intensity over technical proficiency. Before long, Seattle bands including Pearl Jam, Soundgarden and Alice in Chains would join Nirvana at the top of the charts, and high-fashion outlets like Nordstrom and Bloomingdale's would start producing grunge clothing lines.

But as explosive as grunge was, it didn't happen like the Big Bang. It took years to evolve. To the outsider, it might seem strange that a music scene with such magnitude and force took place in a city as conservative and far removed as Seattle. But to understand how grunge changed the music community, it's necessary to understand the musical environment in which its chief contributors were weaned.

Since Seattle hasn't historically been a cultural Mecca, artists seeking fame and fortune have traditionally emigrated elsewhere. Jimi Hendrix was discovered in London, Heart made its mark in Vancouver, Canada, and Queensrÿche had to be declared rock gods in Europe before they were accepted at home. As a result, local musicians generally had to settle for having fun, letting off steam, and maybe getting laid, but few harbored real hopes of becoming rock stars. Because of this, there seemed to be no great need for stellar musicianship.

The tradition of sloppy Seattle garage rock actually began in the Sixties when a group called the Sonics started playing an irreverent, thrashy and energetic style of music that foreshadowed punk. Soon after, a host of like-minded outfits began setting up shop in basements all over town, and creating a furious din that no one but themselves were likely to hear. The trend continued through the Seventies and Eighties, as garage rockers gradually evolved into glam bangers like Whiz Kids and the Lewd, and full-fisted metal bands such as TKO, Metal Church, Forced Entry and, of course, Coven, who crafted the unforgettable underground ditty "Iron Dick."

So what prompted so many seemingly nice kids to pick up guitars and lose their minds? Simple: boredom. Years before grunge, Starbucks and Microsoft hit the area, Seattle was merely a sleepy suburb of Boeing, with plenty of natural beauty but little in the way of quality entertainment. And even the folks who dug salmon fishing, rock climbing and outdoor hikes were limited by the region's miserable weather conditions. Like England, Seattle is cold, cloudy and dreary. Local residents look forward to only about 33 days of cloudless sunshine per year, and even in the summer, the mercury doesn't usually hit the 80 degree mark until after Independence Day. It would probably be a stretch to say that if Seattle had Sacramento's climate, grunge would never have happened, but there's no question that Seattle's weather has caused many bands to stay in the rehearsal room longer than they might have otherwise, and it's certainly contributed to the genre's bleak, cynical lyrics. Anyway, what better way to deal with frustration than to pick up a guitar and scream? The nation's economy was at nearly an all-time low. Students were graduating from college and finding that, if they were lucky, they could maybe find employment at the elevator music company Musak, or at Boeing, unless they wanted to go off into the country to pick apples, that is.

So what exactly is grunge? Well, in its purest form it's definitely grudge music, and it sounds like it's been splattered with scunge, but as a catch phrase, it's somewhat limiting. After all, Nirvana doesn't sound that much like Pearl Jam, who doesn't seem that much like Alice in Chains, who have little in common with Screaming Trees and bears even less similarity to the Fastbacks. As a general guideline, grunge music is stompy, swampy and ultra-distorted, and is perhaps best typified by early Mudhoney or Soundgarden. Picture a supergroup made up of Creedence Clearwater Revival, Black Sabbath and the Stooges, and you're pretty close. Grunge is angry and filled with attitude, but it rarely lacks melody.

To someone unfamiliar with Seattle, it might seem strange that nearly all the great grunge bands were on the same label (Sub Pop), and came from the same general area. But Seattle's a cozy, communal city, the kind of place where everyone knows their neighbors, and the same 100 people show up at nearly every rock gig. In the early days of grunge, the music scene was friendly and unified. Since no one expected to achieve stardom, there wasn't any of the backstabbing and deceit so common with bands in areas like Los Angeles and New York. At one point or another, nearly every musician had jammed with or been in a band with everyone, and there was a genuinely positive spirit about the scene.

There's been plenty of debate over whether grunge derives from punk or heavy metal, but the truth is, the music collectively fuses both music forms. Nirvana, Pearl Jam and especially Soundgarden used to argue that they were heavy, but not metal, yet their sound was unmistakably influenced by Black Sabbath, Led Zeppelin and Motorhead. Sure, the "I-could-give-a-fuck" attitude and introspective lyrics were manifested from alt-punks like the Ramones, Dinosaur Jr and Hüsker Dü, but the "chunka-chunka" rhythms told a different story. In fact, Seattle grunge bands were so metal that by the time Nirvana had released their third album, *In Utero*, one-time metalheads had basically discarded the music they held so dear to embrace this new, vibrant form of noise. Suddenly, bands like Guns N' Roses, Ratt and Mötley Crüe became an anachronism. They were singing about celebration and escapism, and when Nirvana, Pearl Jam and Soundgarden came along, audiences realized that it's better to confront emotional pain than ignore it. Listeners discovered a sensitivity and insecurity in grunge music that they could empathize with. No longer were rock stars putting up an impenetrable wall of bravado. They were letting down their guard, expressing their vulnerability and admitting that, like the rest of us, they were all scared geeks and "losers."

Most Seattle grungologists agree that the Melvins are the missing link that united Seattle's punk and metal primates (which may come as a surprise to those who thought Tad was so big and hairy that he just had to be the bond between punk monkey and metal misanthrope). Their slow, sludgy riffs sounded like Black Sabbath at half speed, and their subversive countenance appealed to true nonconformists in the community. Although the Melvins weren't terribly popular, and never even performed much live, they were hugely influential. In fact, Kurt Cobain and Soundgarden's Chris Cornell have both credited the band with helping shape their sound.

But while the Melvins planted the seeds of grunge, it was a little band called Green River that started the grunge family tree in the mid Eighties. Composed of Mark Arm, Steve Turner, Jeff Ament and Stone Gossard, Green River played a vibrant form of theatrical rock that mixed punk bluster with the aesthetics of glam and the dynamics of metal. Their second recording was one of the first releases on the fledgling label Sub Pop, and its appearance heralded the beginning of something big. In 1987, Green River broke up and its members branched off into two factions. Turner and Arm formed the contentious, swampy punk band Mudhoney, while Ament and Gossard created the bluesy, more commercial Mother Love Bone with consummate showman/vocalist Andrew Wood. When Wood died of a heroin overdose three years later, Ament and Gossard formed Pearl Jam.

1987 was to grunge what 1977 was to punk rock. Soundgarden released its first EP, *Screaming Life*, on Sub Pop, and the attention it attracted helped the label plant its feet in Seattle's sludgy soil. The record was hugely influential for numerous bands including Nirvana and Tad, who both formed that year. Alice in Chains linked up in 1987 as well, but they started out as a commercial glam metal band, and their early material owed more to Queen and Queensrÿche than to the Melvins or Green River.

Before long, the grunge buzz started to spread. Tiny clubs like the Vogue, Squid Row and Central Tavern started booking shows by Nirvana, Soundgarden, Mudhoney, and Mother Love Bone, as well as lesser known acts including Skin Yard (which featured Seattle producer Jack Endino), the Fluid, and Blood Circus. But, at that point, the movement was still underground. When Nirvana frontman Kurt Cobain smirkingly and ironically wrote in Nirvana's first bio, "We want to cash in and suck butt up to the bigwigs in hopes that we too can get high and fuck wax figure hot babes... Soon we will do encores of 'Gloria' and 'Louie Louie' at benefit concerts with all our celebrity friends," he did so with the conviction that Nirvana would remain a cult entity for years, if not for the rest of his music career, two words which at the time seemed like an oxymoron.

In truth, Nirvana wasn't supposed to be Sub Pop's cash cow at first. In the biography *Come As You Are: The Story of Nirvana*, Michael Azerrad wrote that label co-founder Bruce Pavitt initially thought the band was too metallic, and was somewhat reluctant to even sign them. Based on the success of Soundgarden, who had just been signed to a major label deal, the label had placed their bets that Mudhoney would be the band to break through. But while Sub Pop may have misjudged the first race, they would have hit the trifecta over and over. Sub Pop has been called the "Don King of grunge," and the description isn't far off the mark. Pavitt and his partner Jonathan Poneman were music-loving businessmen who heard something in the Seattle music scene that they felt they could cash in on. At first, however, the cash was slow to flow. The two had started the label in 1987 with a $19,000 loan, which they quickly blew on office space, advertising, promotion and distribution. While early records like Mudhoney's *Superfuzz Bigmuff* EP (1988), Tad's ferociously brutal *God's Balls* (1989), and Nirvana's debut, *Bleach* (1989), did respectably enough, the label wasn't officially in the black until after the Mudhoney album, *Every Good Boy Deserves Fudge*, in 1991.

Interestingly, grunge originated in Seattle, but didn't catch on in America until after it became the talk of the town in Britain. Realizing that numerous U.S. acts including Hendrix, Blondie and Faith No More generated interest in England before making waves in America, Sub Pop spent money they didn't really have to fly *Melody Maker* journalist Everett True to Seattle to check out Mudhoney, Tad and Nirvana, and True returned raving about grunge. *Melody Maker*'s vehement praise had a ripple effect across the European press, and after the three bands were sent to London for a brief tour, world domination wasn't far away. *Superfuzz Bigmuff* spent a year on the U.K. indie chart, and the label's seminal compilation *Sub Pop 2,000*, which featured Soundgarden, Tad, Nirvana, Mudhoney, Beat Happening and Screaming Trees, was referred to by Radio One guru, John Peel, as a document of the most important regional music scene since Motown. Before long, the American press started to catch on, and after Nirvana released its outstanding *Bleach* (recorded for a mere $606), Tad and Nirvana embarked on a rigorous, riotous tour that spread the gospel of grunge across the land.

Once music fans wrapped their ears around the writhing rhythms and agonized vocals of *Bleach*, it became obvious that

Nirvana would be the first Sub Pop band to break. But area pundits believed Mother Love Bone would be the band to achieve true rock stardom. Frontman Andrew Wood was a passionate singer and natural ham, and when the group performed, audiences could taste his need to be adored. Between Wood's showmanship and the band's classic rock chops, which were less noisy and more hooky than those of Nirvana, Tad or Mudhoney, Mother Love Bone seemed poised for greatness. But Wood's career was short-lived, and when he died of a heroin overdose in 1990, the task fell on an ambivalent Nirvana to become Seattle's hometown heroes.

The band easily met and exceeded the demand. *Nevermind* (1991), which included the hits "Smells Like Teen Spirit" and "Come As You Are," sold 10 million copies. Pearl Jam followed with the hugely successful hard rock opus *Ten* (1991), which sold millions and reached Number Two on *Billboard*. Soundgarden had its first Platinum album, *Badmotorfinger*, the same year, and soon after, Alice in Chains fuzzed up, slowed down, and hit paydirt with *Dirt* (1992). Before you could say "Touch Me I'm Sick," Seattle was glutted with fuzzbox-stomping bands who had packed their gear and hopped on the grunge rock bandwagon. Many groups actually moved to Seattle from other cities to live out their rock and roll fantasies. Some even included the words "Love," "Bone" or "Garden" in their names in a desperate effort to lend themselves credibility. Groups like Gruntruck, Skin Yard, My Sister's Machine, Love Battery, Hammerbox, Flop, Willard, Treepeople and Monomen began to attract interest, but most of the new breed was second rate.

Singles, a Hollywood film based on the lives of Seattle slackers and musicians, helped make the scene even more mainstream, as did designer grungewear. Then a slew of bands from other regions started playing grunge, figuring, "Gee, why relocate to Seattle to cash in, when I can do it in my own backyard?" Pretty soon, bands like Stone Temple Pilots, Our Lady Peace, Sponge, Everclear, Silverchair, Verve Pipe and Bush entered the picture. But while these bands were able to approximate the volume and aggression of the Seattle sound, they lacked authenticity. They hadn't grown up with the progenitors of the movement or watched the scene evolve from a cult to a phenomenon. They hadn't known or shared jokes with Andrew Wood, Kristen Pfaff or Kurt Cobain while they were still alive, or created side project records with their neighbors. In short, they lacked the camaraderie that united the Seattle grunge community.

At the same time grunge went supernova, its prime movers started to self-destruct. Nirvana began to verbally attack their fans, accusing many of their fratboy followers of being the same kinds of kids who beat them up in high school. Cobain was unwillingly handed the responsibility of being a spokesperson for a generation of confused, disgruntled youth, only he was too confused and disgruntled himself to deal with the pressure. He once told *MTV News* that he wanted to have "the fame of John Lennon and the anonymity of Ringo Starr," but that was an impossibility, and his life turned into a media circus. Since he couldn't cope, he tried to escape with heroin, as did other members of the Seattle community.

Just as Nirvana's ascent symbolized the birth of grunge on a mainstream level, Cobain's death signaled the beginning of the end. Cobain, who had overdosed on heroin numerous times in the past, always seemed to bounce back and perform with amazing passion and acuity. But a few months before the release of *In Utero* it became apparent that his condition was out of control. In May 1993, he overdosed at his Seattle home, but was revived. Less than a month later, he was arrested and charged with domestic assault after having an argument with his wife, Courtney Love, over his gun collection. In July, he overdosed again in the bathroom of his New York hotel room shortly before Nirvana was due on stage to perform at the New Music Seminar. *In Utero* came out in September and immediately rocketed to the top of the charts, but Nirvana was rapidly unraveling, and during a tour of Europe in early March, Love found Cobain in their hotel room, unconscious from an overdose of the tranquilizer Rohypnol. He remained in a coma for 20 hours, and while the incident was initially reported as an accident, a suicide note was found at the scene. For Cobain, the catch phrase "I hate myself and I want to die," the proposed title of *In Utero*, had become a frightening reality.

From there, things spiraled downhill. On March 18, upon returning from Europe, Love was forced to call the police after Cobain locked himself in the bathroom of their home, and threatened to kill himself with a .38 revolver. Two weeks later, after an ugly intervention by his wife, bandmates and friends, Cobain was admitted to the Exodus Recovery Center in Los Angeles. On April 1, he escaped the unit, telling staffers there that he was going outside to smoke a cigarette. Seven days later, he was found in a room above his garage, dead from a self inflicted shotgun wound to the head.

Cobain's death shell-shocked the world, but devastated the Seattle music community. When grunge broke, Seattle rock and roll was supposed to be a celebratory dream, a never-ending party where everyone left drunk and wealthy. Then the dream turned into a nightmare, and suddenly the community sobered up enough to realize the party was no longer worth the cover charge. Weeks after Cobain's suicide, Hole bassist Kristen Pfaff died of a heroin overdose. Almost immediately, bands began distancing themselves from the beast they had created. Sub Pop started signing eccentric bands like Combustible Edison and Red Red Meat, which were far removed from grunge. Pearl Jam stopped doing press and became more political, engaging in a full-throttle battle with Ticketmaster. Alice in Chains released one more album before dropping out of sight without touring to support the record, and Soundgarden started to evolve out of their dense, muddy sound, towards something more melodic and otherworldly.

But perhaps the aftershocks of Cobain's death were too strong to keep even those bands together. In early 1997, Soundgarden broke up because of personal and musical differences. And while Alice in Chains hasn't official announced its demise, guitarist Jerry Cantrell is now working on a solo album with drummer Sean Kinney, and vocalist Layne Staley hasn't been heard from since the band's MTV *Unplugged* performance in 1996.

Today, a nation of post-alternative teens laughs at the memory of grim-faced grunge. Flannel is only worn when it's cold out, and even "Smells Like Teen Spirit" seems as dated to mainstream America as "Born to Be Wild." But scoff as they may, they can't deny the significance grunge has had on the contemporary music scene. Old school metal bands like Metallica and Mötley Crüe have been inspired to craft slower, looser songs laced with harmonies, new metal bands like Tool and Korn have learned that dynamics and creativity are as important as volume and violence, and nearly every alternative band has flat-out nicked Nirvana's soft verse/loud chorus formula at one time or another.

Some critics argue that the parasitic media killed grunge. They say that, like a vampire, the beast came in, sucked the lifeblood from the scene, and then left in search of a new victim. But blaming the demise of grunge on the media is like blaming declining literacy on Nintendo. It's just too simplistic. For many Seattle bands, teenage angst paid off well for a while, but perhaps the weight of that anger and frustration became too ponderous to support the music. Or maybe too many post-Nirvana bands watered down their songs in their bid for commercial success, and music listeners decided to seek out something more visceral. Maybe a nation of youngsters just got tired of all the griping, complaining and self-deprecation, and decided to focus on something positive. Whatever the reason, the grunge scene died because music fans stopped buying grunge records. Like disco, punk, new wave and metal before it, the music ran its course, changing the world for a while, then fizzling away to make room for something new.

Had Cobain known that, he might have stuck around long enough to bask in the afterglow.

NIRVANA

Guitar World, February 1992

Smells Like Teen Idol

Kurt Cobain tries to explain why Nirvana, third-hand guitars and all, is suddenly the hottest band in the country.

By Jeff Gilbert

E'RE JUST MUSICALLY and rhythmically retarded," asserts Kurt Cobain, guitarist, vocalist and chief songwriter for Nirvana. "We play so hard that we can't tune our guitars fast enough. People can relate to that."

Seems reasonable enough, considering that *Nevermind*, the Seattle trio's major label debut, has become one of the hottest out-of-the-box albums in the country. Fueled by the contagious hit single, "Smells Like Teen Spirit," the spirited album turned Gold a mere five weeks after its release, and leaped past both volumes of Guns N' Roses' *Use Your Illusion* just one month later. But its sudden, platinum-bound popularity probably has more to do with the band's infectious, dirty riffs and wry lyrical hooks than with its roughly played, out-of-tune guitars, of which Cobain is so proud.

"We sound like the Bay City Rollers after an assault by Black Sabbath," continues the guitarist in his nasty smoker's hack. "And," he expectorates, "we vomit on stage better than anyone!"

Nirvana began its career with 1989's *Bleach* (Sub Pop), an intensely physical melange of untuned metal, drunk punk and Seventies pop, written from the perspective of a college drop-out. The album's other notable distinction was that it was recorded in three days for

$600. *Nevermind*, costing considerably more than six bills, is Nirvana's major-label, power-punk/pop masterpiece, awash in slashing, ragged guitar riffs, garbled lyrics and more teen spirit than you can shake a Kiss record at.

GUITAR WORLD: MTV thinks Nirvana is a metal band.

KURT COBAIN: That's fine; let them be fooled! I don't have anything against Headbanger's Ball, but it's strange to see our faces on MTV.

GW: [Metallica's] Kirk Hammett is a huge Nirvana fan.

COBAIN: That's real flattering. We met him recently and he's a real nice guy. We talked about the Sub Pop scene, heavy metal and guitars.

GW: Speaking of guitars, you seem to favor low-end models.

COBAIN: I don't favor them—it's just that I can afford them. [*laughs*] I'm left-handed, and it's not very easy to find reasonably priced, high-quality, left-handed guitars. But out of all the guitars in the whole world, the Fender Mustang is my favorite. I've only owned two of them.

GW: What is it about the Mustang that works for you?

COBAIN: They're cheap and totally inefficient, and they sound like crap. They're also very small and don't stay in tune, and when you want to raise the string action on the fretboard, you have to loosen all the strings and completely remove the bridge. You have to turn these little screws with your fingers and hope that you've estimated it right. If you screw up, you have to repeat the process over and over until you get it right. Whoever invented that guitar was a dork.

GW: It was Leo Fender.

COBAIN: I guess I'm calling Leo Fender, the dead guy, a dork. Now I'll never get an endorsement. [*laughs*] We've been offered a Gibson endorsement, but I can't find a Gibson I like.

GW: Is the Mustang your only guitar?

COBAIN: No, I own a '66 Jaguar. That's the guitar I polish and baby—I refuse to let anyone touch it when I jump into the crowd. [*laughs*] Lately, I've been using a Strat live, because I don't want to ruin my Mustang yet. I like to use Japanese Strats because they're a bit cheaper, and the frets are smaller than the American version's.

GW: The acoustic guitar you play on "Polly" sounds flat.

COBAIN: That's a 20-dollar junk shop Stella—I didn't bother changing the strings. [*laughs*] It barely stays in tune. In fact, I have to use duct tape to hold the tuning keys in place.

GW: Considering how violently you play the guitar, you probably use pretty heavy-duty strings.

COBAIN: Yeah. And I keep blowing up amplifiers, so I use whatever I can find at junk shops—junk is always best.

GW: What was the last amp you blew up?

COBAIN: A Crown power amp that was intended for use as a PA, but which I used for a guitar head because I can never find an amp that's powerful enough—and because I don't want to have to deal with hauling 10 Marshall heads. I'm lazy—I like to have it all in one package. For a preamp I have a Mesa/Boogie, and I turn all the mid-range up. And I use Radio Shack speakers.

GW: How reliable is this set-up? It doesn't seem like it would be that durable, especially in view of all the touring you do.

COBAIN: It works out okay. The sound changes with every club we play in, but I'm never satisfied. I think the sound I get is mainly a result of the Roland EF-1 distortion box I use. I go through about five a tour.

GW: Ever get the urge to use a twang bar?

COBAIN: No. Anybody that plays guitar knows that only Jimi Hendrix was able to use the standard tremolo and still keep it in tune. Those things are totally worthless. I do have one on a Japanese Strat, but I don't use it.

GW: Your first album, *Bleach*, was recorded for $600; how much did *Nevermind* run you?

COBAIN: [*laughs*] I don't remember; I've got Alzheimer's. And don't ask us how much our video cost; that's a hell of an embarrassment.

KURT COBAIN of NIRVANA

Guitar World, July 1994

Cast a Giant Shadow

Kurt Cobain—rock visionary, godfather of grunge, voice of the disaffected—was also a powerful and influential guitarist. Alan di Perna discusses his impact on American music—and why a man who had everything came to the terrible conclusion that he had nothing.

By Alan di Perna

OST OF US think of failure as the main motive for suicide. That's what makes it so hard to accept the sad and senseless death of Kurt Cobain. Musically speaking, he was a resounding success. Cobain had attained the very things that many readers of this magazine are striving for right now: chart topping records, phenomenal popularity, wealth and—most important—the respect of his peers and millions of rock fans. As the leader of Nirvana, Kurt Cobain set the tone for rock music in the Nineties. Considerable symbolic importance can be found in the way Nirvana's *Nevermind* booted Michael Jackson off the charts in 1991, signaling the end of the Eighties and ushering in the style of raw, guitar-heavy, blunt-spoken rock that so far has dominated this decade.

But Nirvana's enormous success was something that Cobain never sought and was certainly never comfortable with. As he declared in the sardonic "Radio Friendly Unit Shifter" (*In Utero*), "I do not want what I have got." A misfit within the institution called Rock and Roll, Cobain personified the anxieties and frustrations of his generation. His death—at age 27, of an apparently self-inflicted wound to the head with a 12-gauge shotgun—has saddened everyone who follows modern rock.

Born on February 20, 1967, Cobain was just eight when his parents divorced. Although almost universally associated with Seattle, he was actually from Aberdeen, Washington, a small, economically depressed logging town more than 100 miles from Seattle. "White trash posing as middle class," is how Cobain described his background to biographer Michael Azerrad in the latter's *Come As You Are: The Story of Nirvana.* By all accounts, Kurt was deeply and permanently hurt by his parents' divorce. After the split, he never really had a stable childhood home. At school he was diagnosed as hyperactive and given the drug Ritalin. He dropped out in the 12th grade. Cobain didn't fit in with the macho stereotype imposed on young males in Aberdeen. He had no use for hunting, sports or other "manly" pursuits, although he did enjoy getting high with the local stoners. He was harassed at high school for befriending a gay student. In later life, he would speak out vehemently against homophobia, sexism and racism.

Cobain demonstrated artistic ability at an early age, and his collages, sculptures and other artworks adorn many of Nirvana's records. Had he not become a musician, he might well have pursued a career in the visual arts. But when he was 14, his fate took another course: his father bought him his first electric guitar, which Kurt soon discovered he was most comfortable playing left-handed. Cobain's musical tastes developed along much the same lines as many musicians of his generation. His mother introduced him to the Beatles, the Monkees and other Sixties pop music when he was very young, but he moved on to bands like Led Zeppelin, Black Sabbath and AC/DC while still in his preteens. When punk rock finally made its way out to Aberdeen, sometime in the early Eighties, Cobain embraced it eagerly. Years later, Kurt would be embarrassed when relatives or childhood friends recalled him jamming to Iron Maiden records or drawing the Led Zeppelin logo on his bedroom wall. But it is precisely that combination of heavy metal and early-Eighties punk (Black Flag, Flipper, etc.) that would later become known as grunge and have an extraordinarily powerful effect on the masses.

Cobain started writing songs soon after picking up the guitar. His first band, a trio called Fecal Matter, did not last long. But in 1986, he and bassist Krist Novoselic, a friend from Aberdeen High, teamed up to form the nucleus of a band that would eventually be called Nirvana. (Cobain had wanted to call it Skid Row at one point.)

By 1987, Cobain had moved to Olympia, Washington, a college town that was somewhat more bohemian than Aberdeen and about 50 miles closer to Seattle. Acquaintances from that time recall him as a quiet, reclusive guy who mainly stayed inside the apartment he shared with his girlfriend, working on his sculptures and collages. An inveterate haunter of thrift shops and swap meets, Cobain was perpetually buying old dolls and other semi-collectible junk, much of which he used in his artwork. He applied his thrift-shop aesthetic to his guitars as well, and became infamous for playing a succession of battered old pawn-shop specials. But there was a practical angle to his obsession with six-string castoffs: affordable left-handed guitars are fairly hard to find and Cobain played with such angry violence that his Fender Jaguars and Jazzmasters—his guitars of choice—frequently needed replacing. In the days before the guitars were popularized by bands like Sonic Youth, Dinosaur Jr—and Nirvana—Jags and Jazzmasters could be had for very reasonable prices. Ultimately, of course, the guitar became more desirable and thus more expensive. Shortly before his death, Cobain designed a signature model hybrid cross between a Jaguar and a Mustang for Fender.

Early in 1988, Cobain, Novoselic and drummer Dale Crover journeyed to Seattle to make a demo at Reciprocal Recording Studios with engineer Jack Endino, an important figure at the city's highly influential indie label, Sub Pop. The demo led to a deal with Sub Pop, and on June 11, 1988, with Chad Channing now on drums, Nirvana released its first single, "Love Buzz," a cover of an obscure song by Shocking Blue, the early-Seventies Dutch group that had had a big hit with "Venus." A year later, Nirvana's first album,

Bleach, came out on Sub Pop.

Cobain often said in interviews that he deliberately suppressed his more melodic, quirky, "new wave" side on *Bleach*. (Kurt often used the term "new wave" to describe everything from the Young Marble Giants and Gang of Four to the Butthole Surfers and Scratch Acid, all groups that had greatly influenced him.) His feeling was that this sensibility didn't really fit in with Sub Pop's early-Seventies hard-rock aesthetic, as exemplified by Soundgarden and Green River, the group which later mutated into Pearl Jam.

Cobain's musical tastes were quite a bit broader than the noisy alternative fare championed by Sub Pop and similar indie labels. But coming from the rural wastelands of a place like Aberdeen, he could see where Nirvana fit in. "We're a perfect example of the average uneducated 'twentysomething' in America in the Nineties," Cobain told Michael Azerrad. "[We're] punk rockers who weren't into punk rock when it was thriving. All my life, that's been the case, because when I got into the Beatles, the Beatles had been broken up for years and I didn't know it... Same thing with Led Zeppelin."

But Cobain's sense of kinship with his age group went beyond music: "My story is exactly the same as 90 percent of everyone my age," he said. "Everyone's parents got divorced. Their kids smoked pot all through high school, they grew up during the era when there was a massive Communist threat and everyone thought they were going to die from a nuclear war. And everyone's personalities are practically the same."

Cobain has been called a reluctant, unwilling spokesman for his generation. But then, it is hard to imagine even the most eager prophet proclaiming, "Hello, I'm the spokesman for my entire generation." In bygone days, Bob Dylan always shrugged off that "spokesman" hype, and John Lennon actively discouraged it. So maybe it's more accurate to say that Cobain was uneasy with notoriety—even the underground notoriety that Nirvana gained on the strength of *Bleach* and its followup EP, *Blew*, also released in 1989. On the band's first European tour, a grueling, low-budget trek with the band Tad, Cobain had what Sub Pop co-owner Bruce Pavitt has described as a nervous breakdown on stage in Rome, storming off stage, climbing into the rafters and screaming at the audience. Adding considerably to Cobain's unhappiness was his chronic, undiagnosable stomach pain, which began shortly after his move to Olympia and would torture him for the rest of his life.

But Kurt's life wasn't completely dark. In 1990, Cobain began a relationship with Tobi Vail, of the band Bikini Kill, a leader in the radical feminist riot *grrrl* movement. He apparently took his relationship seriously; by all accounts, he wasn't much of a casual womanizer. He told Michael Azerrad that he only slept with two women over the course of all Nirvana's touring. "I've always been old-fashioned in that respect," he said. "I've always wanted a girlfriend that I could have a good relationship with for a long time. I wish I was capable of just playing the field, but I always wanted more than that."

Another key person who entered the Nirvana circle around this time was their new drummer, Dave Grohl. An explosive, hard-hitting stickman, Grohl took Nirvana's sound to a new level of intensity. He joined the band just in time for their signing to Geffen Records, a deal that was facilitated to a large degree by Sonic Youth's Thurston Moore, who had recently signed with the label. Cobain, Novoselic and Grohl teamed up with producer Butch Vig to record what was to become a landmark rock album, 1991's *Nevermind*. Once again, Cobain decided to rein in his arty tendencies toward pop melodicism, fearing that they would be perceived as sellout elements occasioned by the band's move to a major label. After the record was completed, he also feared that Andy Wallace's mix was a little *too* radio-friendly. "Looking back on the production of *Nevermind*, I'm a little embarrassed by it," he told Azerrad. "It's closer to a Mötley Crüe record than it is to a punk rock record."

Understandable though they may be, Cobain's artistic qualms about the record sell it short. It is an astoundingly powerful album, an irrefutable declaration of an important new band's arrival. The disc's first single, "Smells Like Teen Spirit," became an instant anthem. It is a showcase for the kind of expressive mood swings that were a trademark of Cobain's guitar playing, songwriting and personality. The tune is a brilliant evocation of volatile emotions, with its sullen, world-weary verses that explode into abrasive power chording for the choruses.

Cobain worked notoriously fast as a lyricist. He'd write the words to his songs in the car on the way to the studio or even a few seconds before having to record a final vocal. But the unstudied, hasty quality of his lyrics are part of their expressiveness. His songs are like action paintings—kinetic, disconnected bursts of angry energy. He shifts from topic to topic in a manner that has been compared to a restless adolescent channel-surfing through the cable TV wasteland. It has been pointed out that Cobain's lyrics were inseparable from his plaintive, raspy vocal style. Nobody else could sing those words with quite the same effect. But it's equally true that Cobain's distinctive voice was inseparable from his guitar style. The voice and guitar in Nirvana rubbed against one another in an ever-shifting dynamic, like a couple making love, or fighting, or both at the same time, with Cobain's choppy guitar rhythms and grainy distortion welling up to dominate at one moment then slipping into subaqueous quietude the next.

The months following the release of *Nevermind* were turbulent ones for Cobain. Not only were there the pressures of sudden, massive stardom to cope with, but he also entered into two relationships that were to have a profound effect on him. One was with Courtney Love, longtime punk scenester and splashy frontwoman for the group Hole. The other was with heroin. Cobain and Love first met at a Nirvana club gig in 1989, but didn't become serious about each other until '91, after Kurt had moved to Los Angeles to record *Nevermind*. Love was often blamed for introducing Cobain to heroin, but he had experimented with the drug as early as his Aberdeen days. Cobain always insisted that he became a serious heroin user of his own accord, because it was the only thing that seemed to quell the terrible pain in his stomach. His description of this pain to Azerrad proved tragically prophetic: "Halfway through [*Nirvana's last*] European tour, I remember saying, 'I'll never go on tour again until I have this fixed' because I wanted to kill myself. I wanted to fucking blow my head off, I was so tired of it."

Cobain and Love were married on February 24, 1992. Their daughter, Francis Bean Cobain, was born on August 18 of that same year. Because of press reports—inaccurate, Love insisted—that she used heroin while pregnant, the Los Angeles Children's Services began proceedings to take the Cobains' daughter away from them. It was the beginning of a long and difficult legal battle that the couple ultimately won, in March of 1993. But it wasn't only the law that seemed to have it in for the Cobains. Provocative, outspoken and confrontational, Love was disliked by many Nirvana fans who perceived her as a golddigger who manipulated the passive Cobain. Love often joked about being her generation's Yoko Ono.

But even in the midst of all these difficulties, Nirvana's career kept on skyrocketing, and Cobain continued developing as a songwriter. December '92 saw the release of *Incesticide*, a collection of previously unreleased rarities. The selections go back to that first Jack Endino-produced demo and tunes like "Hairspray Queen" and "Mexican Seafood." The public finally got to hear some of the "new wave" side that Cobain had suppressed on *Bleach* and *Nevermind*. Meanwhile, at a much more advanced level, Cobain was writing songs for what would become Nirvana's final, and arguably finest, album, *In Utero*. Thanks to the band's success, Cobain was finally able to make pretty much the album he'd always wanted to make. The result is a far more diverse and adventurous album than *Nevermind*. Cobain's songwriting skills had become more focused and assured. "Serve the Servants" verges on the Beatlesque, while "Scentless Apprentice" is among the heaviest things Nirvana ever recorded. Tracks like "Rape Me," "Heart Shaped Box" and the stately "Pennyroyal Tea" showcased Cobain's unique sense of melodic phrasing: vocal lines of irregular length that generally resolved on the major third of whatever chord the singer happened to be strumming when the line ended. Cobain's words and cover art suggest a peacefully resigned acceptance of the life cycle, from birth to death. Even the album's more disturbing images of disease and pain seem appropriate elements of that cycle.

If only Cobain's personal life had been similarly harmonious. The sad chain of events leading to his death probably began on March 4, 1994, in Rome, when Cobain fell into a near-fatal coma after taking some 60 sedative pills washed down with champagne. Although initially reported as an accident, the *Los Angeles Times* later stated that the overdose was in fact a suicide attempt and that Cobain had even left a suicide note. (The newspaper cited "sources close to the situation who asked not to be identified" as the basis for this statement.) Two weeks later, police were summoned to Cobain and Love's home in Seattle. Cobain had locked himself in a room with three or four guns (reports vary) and 25 boxes of ammunition, following a quarrel with his wife, who called in the law because she feared he intended to take his life. Cobain denied this, saying he merely wanted to be alone for a while. The officers confiscated his weapons, nevertheless. Cobain had begun to amass a collection of guns—for protection purposes, he said—while he and Love were living in Los Angeles.

By March 28, Cobain and Love had returned to L.A., she to work out some final details on the release of Hole's new album, *Live Through This*, he to check into a drug rehabilitation clinic. This was to be the last of several unsuccessful rehab attempts. Three days later, Cobain abruptly left the clinic and apparently flew back to Seattle. Fearing for his safety, Love hired private detectives who tried in vain to locate him. On the morning of April 8, his body was found at a home he owned in Seattle. An electrician who had come to work on the premises made the discovery. Medical experts determined that Cobain had been dead for several days.

Shortly before the death, it was reported that Nirvana planned to break up. In his suicide note, Cobain said, "I haven't felt excitement in listening to as well as creating music for too many years now. I feel guilty beyond words about these things." The note goes on to thank Nirvana's fans for their "letters and concern during the last years."

Among the many ironies associated with this brilliant artist's short, sad life is that while he was unable to conquer his own intense pain, his music helped millions of fans deal with theirs.

Guitar World, March 1995

Season Finale

A behind-the-scenes look at Nirvana's brilliant performance on MTV's *Unplugged.*

By Alan di Perna

HE IMAGES HAVE already been burned into some deep, tender part of rock's collective consciousness: Kurt Cobain, slumped over his Martin acoustic, his tattered librarian sweater and basketball sneakers, the clusters of lilies, the subaquatic blue light...

Who can say why MTV chose to air Nirvana's *Unplugged* performance over and over, like a tape loop, in the hours and days following the discovery of Cobain's lifeless body on April 8, 1994? Many fans might have preferred some bracing footage of Nirvana fully amped up and defiantly live before a seething mosh pit. Instead, there was Nirvana *Unplugged*, taped just five months before Cobain's death, selected as the focal point for the rock community's grief and shock. The recent release of Nirvana's *MTV Unplugged in New York*, the CD version of the television concert, was a mournful déjà vu experience for many. It has become impossible to hear this music outside the context of Cobain's terrible end.

Seen, again and again, in the hours after the artist's death, the somber MTV gig had an oddly lulling effect. It may have helped some viewers find a calm, quiet way to resign themselves to Cobain's violent departure. But the effect was pretty spooky, too. It was as if the guy was singing at his own funeral. Or singing to us from some tranquil, blue world beyond our own.

An eerie coincidence? Probably. But of the six cover songs Cobain chose to sing that evening, five mention death in some way. And the lilies, candles and heavy drapery that adorned the *Unplugged* set that night were all chosen by Cobain. In fact, when *Unplugged* producer Alex Coletti showed the Nirvana leader some preliminary sketches for the stage set, Kurt called for more flowers, more candles.

"You mean like a funeral?" Coletti asked.

"Yeah," replied Cobain.

"I don't want to read too much into it," says Coletti in retrospect, "but that memory sure spooked me out a couple of months later."

Apart from any of the show's real or imaginary morbid overtones, for Cobain, the opportunity to do *MTV Unplugged* may well have meant the confirmation of his arrival as an important rock songwriter. "I'm embarrassed saying this, but I'd like to be recognized more as a songwriter," Cobain told *Details* magazine in November of '93. "I don't pay attention to polls and charts, but I thumb through them once in while and see, like, Eddie Vedder is nominated number-one songwriter in some magazine, and I'm not even listed."

From its debut broadcast back in January of 1990, *MTV Unplugged* has always been a songwriters' forum. The show gives tunesmiths an opportunity to strip away the high decibels and big production values and let their compositions stand on their own melodic and lyrical integrity. In 1993, Nirvana had begun working some acoustic numbers into their live set, "just to wind things down," Nirvana bassist Chris Novoselic told *MTV News*. "But people still manage to writhe around and throw shoes and land headfirst over the barrier and crack their heads open."

Unplugged gave Nirvana a chance to test its acoustic mettle under slightly more favorable conditions. "I was surprised but delighted when they said yes to doing the show," says Coletti. Coletti had worked with Nirvana once before. On January 10, 1992, when Nirvana was in New York City to do *Saturday Night Live*, he had videotaped a live set with the band. "Various clips from that have been aired on MTV," Coletti notes, "but never the whole thing. There were 10 or 11 songs, and there's stuff like 'Molly's Lips,' 'Stain,' and other great stuff that's never been seen."

The January '92 taping was an impromptu session, knocked together at the last minute, but it gave Coletti some useful insights into the band. "That one experience of working with Kurt showed me how sensitive he was as a person. Some bands will just walk in and it's like, 'Whatever. Point and shoot. Let's do it and get out of here.' But Kurt seemed to like to take things and internalize them. I'd heard that he was something of a visual artist. So, beyond making sure he was happy with the stage set, since he seemed to show some interest in it, I thought it would be good if he had some creative input into it."

Early in the planning stages of their *Unplugged* appearance, Nirvana tour managers Alex MacLeod and Jeff Mason acted as intermediaries between Cobain and Coletti, passing the guitarist's ideas and wishes on to the producer. "Kurt wanted something that would break away from just the normal, dull TV set," says MacLeod. "He didn't want it to look like just a bare stage. He had seen a lot of *Unplugged* shows before, and felt they weren't really unplugged. His feeling was that a lot of the bands would just use semi-acoustic instruments and play their songs exactly the same way they would if they were doing a full show. He wanted to make Nirvana's *Unplugged* appearance slightly different, sort of a downbeat kind of set. Really laid back. To just go in and play a bunch of songs and make changes to the arrangements to some extent. They tried to stick to acoustic instruments as much as possible. Kurt wanted to make it something that would show a whole different side of the band."

After exchanging these preliminary ideas through MacLeod and Mason, Coletti felt the time was ripe for a face-to-face meeting with Cobain. In November of '93, a few weeks before the taping, Coletti flew up to a Nirvana gig in a remote part of New England, somewhere north of Boston. He was armed with rough sketches of the stage set which embodied Cobain's ideas, and with his own personal Ovation semi-acoustic bass guitar. The latter was meant to be loaned to Chris

Novoselic in the event that the Nirvana bassist didn't have an "Unplugged bass" of his own.

"It was not a glamorous backstage by any means," Coletti recalls. "The show was in a high school hockey arena. After the show, the band went back to this room and had a catered meal. It was nothing fancy, just franks and beans and a bottle of wine. There were a good dozen people in the room: the band and some friends. So I just got thrown in this room and sat down next to Kurt. No one even bothered to introduce us or anything; it was sort of an awkward situation. So I said, 'Is this a bad time? Do you want to do this now or what?' But he immediately became very friendly, like, 'Oh, oh, the MTV thing. No, let's do it now.' I was prepared to give him the whole *Unplugged* spiel, which is to talk about set lists, sound equipment and things. But it just seemed like it wasn't the right time. So I simply said, 'Hey look, I've got some set drawings.' "

Like many people who worked with Cobain in a professional capacity, Coletti describes the late guitarist as a courteous collaborator, respectful of other people's expertise and quietly hopeful of being respected in turn. "He gave us flexibility. He was pretty cooperative," says Coletti. "He did specify that he wanted star lilies, which are these big, white flowers."

It was at this meeting that the ominous "funeral" remark went down. But before anyone could dwell on it, Chris Novoselic burst into the room brandishing the Ovation bass Coletti had left for him. "He was like, 'Look what I got!' Like a big kid," Coletti narrates. "Kurt just looks up and says, 'That's the ugliest fucking thing I've ever seen in my life.' Chris is like, 'Oh, man, I wanna use it on the show.' Kurt said, 'Well, maybe if we fuck it up and bash it up and put some stickers on it...' And I went, 'Umm, you can't do that, Kurt. That's mine!' He got really apologetic, like, 'I'm sorry. I didn't really mean the ugly crack.' "

The set list was another point of discussion, if not contention, between Nirvana and MTV. There were two potential sore points between the parties. First, the band wanted to fill nearly half of their set with obscure covers. "Right away," recalls Alex MacLeod, "we started sorting out how many covers there would be time for, how many songs MTV wanted them to do in total. Just general things like that."

Also disturbing for MTV was the fact that—with the exception of "Come As You Are"—the band wasn't planning to perform any big, instantly recognizable Nirvana hits. "We knew we didn't want to do an acoustic version of 'Teen Spirit,' " drummer Dave Grohl later commented. "That would've been horrendously stupid. We felt it would be better if we found other songs."

According to MacLeod, there was also a practical side to the band's decision not to perform many hits: "They were like, 'We'd love to do that, but a lot of those songs are really dull if we do them that way. They didn't really work acoustically.' The band just thought that there were other songs better-suited to the acoustic format."

The decision to do so many covers reflects a selfless (perhaps insecure) desire on Cobain's part to share the spotlight with other songwriters. He was a tireless proselytizer for bands he really loved, like the Vaselines, Scottish buzz-pop supremos led by Eugene Kelly, who now fronts the band Eugenius. Nirvana had covered Vaselines tunes in the past, including "Molly's Lips" and "Son of a Gun." [These early recordings were later collected on the *Incesticide* CD.] For *Unplugged* he performed the Vaselines' "Jesus Doesn't Want Me for a Sunbeam," which also took on eerie overtones when the show re-aired after his suicide.

The Meat Puppets were another of Kurt's obsessions. "He told me the second Meat Puppets album was great," Cobain's widow, Courtney Love, recalled in a December '94 interview with *Rolling Stone*. "I couldn't stand [the album]. Then he played [those songs] to me—his voice, his cadence and his timing. And I realized he was right. I got to sit and listen to this man serenade me."

Thanks to *Unplugged*, Cobain's fans got a chance to replicate Love's experience. Kurt's performance of the Puppets' "Plateau," "Oh Me" and "Lake of Fire" have a ragged vulnerability that's far more personal and affecting than any calculated run-through of "Teen Spirit" could have been. In retrospect, there was solid wisdom in Coletti's decision to weather his MTV superiors' pressure to see Nirvana play its hits and honor Cobain's intentions instead.

"Kurt said he really enjoyed those Meat Puppets songs because he really had to push his voice," Coletti observes. "Like he didn't feel good singing them. He picked them purposely because they were challenging vocally for him."

Many of the decisions about songs and arrangements went down at two day-long rehearsals held prior to the day of taping. "They were at the SST rehearsal facility in New Jersey," Alex MacLeod recalls. "We brought our own monitor system in. Also, because we were on tour at the time, they were working on stuff during soundcheck. Kurt worked on his own, too."

Since the Meat Puppets were on tour with Nirvana at the time, and Cobain was planning to sing three of their tunes, it seemed a natural move to invite the two principal Puppets, siblings Curt and Cris Kirkwood, to come lend a hand on acoustic guitars. "Why not?" Novoselic later quipped. "We weren't learning their songs right anyway."

Back at MTV HQ, the decision to include the Meat Puppets in the broadcast was hardly greeted with jubilation. Alex Coletti recalls: "I said to MTV, 'They're going to bring some guests on.' And at first everybody's eyes lit up, like, 'Who's it gonna be?' They wanted to hear the 'right' names'—Eddie Vedder or Tori Amos or God knows who. But when I said, 'the Meat Puppets,' it was kind of like, 'Oh great. They're not doing any hits, and they're inviting guests who don't have any hits to come play. Perfect.' "

Nirvana seemed intent on bringing sonic variety to their set. Along with the Kirkwood brothers, they also included cellist Lori Goldston and former Germs guitarist Pat Smear, both of whom had been playing with Nirvana on their tour. Covering the Vaselines' "Jesus Doesn't Want Me for a Sunbeam" gave Chris Novoselic a chance to put down his bass and strap on an accordion. The accordion, he told MTV News, "was the first instrument I learned when I was young. And Kurt bought one, this really neat red one. And I go, 'Hey, check this out.' And I put it on and started playing it. And then we were starting to screw around with rehearsals for *Unplugged* and we did 'Jesus Doesn't Want Me for a Sunbeam.' There's this violin or organ [on the original recording] and I go, 'I know. I'll play the accordion in this song!' I picked it up and started playing, and it sounded really cool."

Despite the band's preparations, Alex MacLeod describes their overall mood as "nervous" as the day of the show approached: "It was the first time in a long while I'd seen them all so nervous about doing something. Things had gotten to the point where they'd go out playing in front of 7,500 or 10,000 people and it was just like [very nonchalantly], 'Okay, boom, let's do it.' But they were really nervous about doing *Unplugged*, because they were really leaving themselves wide open."

As Alex Coletti remembers it, Dave Grohl and Chris Novoselic were the first to turn up at Sony Music Studios, at 54th Street and 10th Avenue in Manhattan, on November 18th, 1993. It was around 3:00 in the afternoon, the appointed time for *Unplugged*'s pre-show camera rehearsal/soundcheck. Concerned with Grohl's propensity to hit the drums really hard, Coletti presented him with some brushes and sizzle sticks, a type of stick used in classical percussion, consisting of several slender dowels loosely wrapped and providing a softer impact than a solid drumstick. Since it was around the holiday season, Coletti had the sticks wrapped up in Christmas paper. "I figured I'd be remembered forever as the dick MTV producer," Coletti laughs. "I was afraid Dave would just roll his eyes, like, 'oh great, the asshole from MTV is trying to be my friend.' But instead he opened the package and said, 'Cool, I've never had brushes before. I've never even tried using them.' As it turned out, he used both the sticks and the brushes, which helped [audio producer] Scott Litt out immensely, I believe. It's nice that the band was so amenable to trying new things."

In the end, Novoselic didn't use Coletti's Ovation bass, but rather a Guild semi-acoustic bass guitar rented from S.I.R. in New York—an instrument that has been used on other episodes of *Unplugged*. Pat Smear played an inexpensive, red-white-and-blue Buck Owens model guitar that belongs to Novoselic and had been extensively reworked by Nirvana guitar technician Earnie Bailey "to get it to sound like a guitar and not a kid's toy," as Alex MacLeod puts it.

Up in the sound booth sat noted record producer Scott Litt (R.E.M., John Mellencamp), who had remixed two tracks from *In Utero* and worked with Nirvana on MTV's *Live and Loud New Years' Eve* show. (Litt went on to produce the Nirvana *Unplugged in New York* CD.) The band and cellist Lori Goldston were already onstage when Cobain arrived, notably unaccompanied by Courtney. "I think that was planned," says Alex Coletti. "I think he was a little too nervous to have Courtney and the baby there."

For the show, Cobain played a Martin D-18E that he had purchased at Voltage Guitar in Los Angeles during the fall of '93, and which had become his main acoustic. With his characteristic flair for the oddball, the guitarist had picked up a rare misfit. The D-18E, one of Martin's earliest stabs at an electrified guitar, is essentially a D-18 acoustic with two pickups, three control knobs and a selector switch grafted on. Introduced in 1958, it was discontinued in 1959; only 302 were ever produced. The instrument was the perfect acoustic (sort of) counterpart to the trashed old Mustangs and Jaguars, the thrift shop clothes and doll parts that Cobain befriended during his brief lifetime.

But this particular castoff had significant cash value: "I don't believe he had any idea how rare it was before he bought it," says Earnie Bailey. "Kurt was neither a collector nor a connoisseur of rare guitars. I think he saw [the D-18E] as an oddity, hoping it would sound as good as it looked. Unfortunately, the instrument's DeArmond pickups were designed with nickel strings in mind, so hearing it with bronze-wound strings was pretty disappointing. Our solution was to attach yet another pickup—a Bartolini model 3AV—to the top of the Martin. Kurt first became interested in [the Bartolini pickup] when he saw Peter Buck using one and really liked the sound."

While the usual *Unplugged* procedure is for acoustic guitars to run direct, Cobain insisted on putting his Martin through his trusty Fender Twin Reverb amp and his usual array of effects boxes. "Maybe

I shouldn't give this secret away," Alex Coletti laughs, "but I built a fake box out in front of the amp to make it look like a monitor wedge. It was Kurt's security blanket. He was used to hearing this guitar through his Fender. He wanted those effects. You can hear it on "The Man Who Sold the World" [*the David Bowie song covered by Nirvana on* Unplugged]. It's an acoustic guitar, but obviously he's going through an amp. There's no trying to pull the wool over anybody's eyes. I actually fought pretty hard to leave that song out [of the final edit of the show]. Because I felt it wasn't as genuine as the rest of the songs. But I'm a huge Bowie fan, so I couldn't fight too hard against the song."

As a concession to the *Unplugged* aesthetic, Earnie Bailey did modify the amp for the show: "To keep the Twin as clean as possible, I switched the 7025 power tubes to 12AX7s and substituted the 12AT7 phase inverter to a 12AU7. By the time Kurt showed up, everything was pretty much dialed in, right down to listening to the pickup balance from the control room."

It is standard *Unplugged* procedure to videotape the camera rehearsal/soundcheck for each show. Nirvana's *Unplugged* rehearsal tape is packed with revelations. More than anything else, Cobain looks tired. His face reflects that unmistakable road weariness that takes hold of musicians after months and months of dealing with strange places, strange situations and even stranger people. Throughout the rehearsal, Cobain's mood varies from low-keyed bitchiness over technical foul-ups to a kind of deadpan, humorous take on the whole proceeding. He calls the second number of the rehearsal, "About a Girl," to an abrupt halt, demanding, "How many more times is that fuckin' feedback gonna happen when I turn my head to the left?" Later on he calls for Finger-Eze to help him smooth out the song's solo: "You know that goofy-ass stuff? It's like anal gel." He later explains that he'd never used the fretboard lubricant before, but that his "country-and-western aunt" used to do so. He nevertheless knows enough to specify that he wants the roll-on rather than the spray. "God, I'm being picky today," he says with mock self-derision.

The whole band seem mildly amused at receiving the superstar treatment from MTV. "Uh, my candle went out. Can somebody please light it?" Dave Grohl demands at one point with stagey hyper-professionalism. "This fucking sand is ridiculous," Cobain says of the substance in which the candelabra and vases were anchored.

What also comes across unmistakably on the videotape is the extent to which Cobain was in charge of Nirvana. He tells Dave Grohl when he's singing flat and directs him to play louder at several junctures. He directs Pat Smear to not keep changing his amp volume. And although he is known for the punkish nonchalance of his guitar approach, the rehearsal tape shows that Cobain could be quite obsessive about tone and guitar equipment. He enters into a lengthy debate with one technician over the various qualities of his two Electro-Harmonix Echo Flangers. Later he asks about the feasibility of acquiring replacement machine heads for his Martin. "These aren't good machine heads," he sadly observes.

As the rehearsal progresses, the trouble spots in the set soon become obvious. One is the aforementioned "Man Who Sold the World." Cobain can't seem to get past the first chorus without blowing the chord changes. "Sorry," he tells the others. The band tries the song again and again, but never manages to get all the way through it. In the end they decide to move on.

"What should we do next, Scott?" shouts Cobain into the darkness above his head. Of all the people on the set, Litt is the only one to whom he seems to defer. The band moves on to a flawless performance of "Polly" and gets halfway through "Dumb" before a monitor snafu again brings things to a halt. "MTV *Poltergeist*," Cobain quips. Trouble rears its ugly head once more when they move on to "Pennyroyal Tea." Pat Smear persists in resolving his chorus harmony vocal to a flagrantly wrong note. Again, the band attempts the song repeatedly, with no success. They try it with Grohl playing Smear's guitar so he can concentrate on his harmony. That doesn't work either. The situation grows painfully reminiscent of the infamous "Well, fuck me, Reg" Troggs rehearsal tape, bootleg copies of which used to circulate among musicians. Once more, the band decides to move on without resolving the problem.

"Jesus Doesn't Want Me for a Sunbeam" comes off infinitely better. But Cobain still seems uneasy. He calls out for someone named Amy (perhaps the Amy Finnerty mentioned in the *Unplugged* CD liner notes): "Amy, can you sit in the front when we play?" Cobain asks. "You and Janet and everyone I know? [*Presumably Janet Billig, from Nirvana's management company.*] 'Cause I hate strangers."

The onstage arrival of "The Brothers Meat" lightens the mood considerably. Their three numbers go well, and the rehearsal closes with a confident reading of "All Apologies." Nirvana leaves the stage having assayed 11 of the 14 songs in their set.

According to Alex MacLeod, the post-soundcheck vibe was fairly tense: "They were still like, 'Oh my God, we haven't rehearsed enough. Oh shit, we're gonna blow this totally.' " After leaving the stage, the band retired to a room upstairs at the Sony facility for a two-hour dinner break. Over the meal, the delicate question of the set list again presented itself. Alex Coletti narrates: "There was this whole subtext of 'try to get Kurt to do more hit songs' that prevailed throughout the day among myself, my boss and management. The other thing was we were really pressuring Scott Litt, like, 'Hey, see if you can get more songs out of them, or better songs.' Again, I'm not saying it was the right thing to do. I think what we got was great. Kurt just chose to take a different road with it. I guess it wasn't the road we were all in synch on. Not that he went in a bad direction at all."

At 8:30 that evening, the audience was "loaded in," as they say at MTV. As it turned out, many of the front row seats were given to New York-area Nirvana fan club members—probably not familiar faces to Cobain, but far from hostile ones. Taping began at nine. Somehow, magically, the rough spots from soundcheck simply seemed to vanish. "I guarantee you I will screw this song up," Cobain nervously announces before starting "The Man Who Sold the World." But he doesn't. The "Pennyroyal Tea" problem resolves itself nicely too. "Am I doing this by myself or what?" Cobain demands. "Do it yourself," Dave Grohl calls out, deftly seizing the opportunity. This impromptu arrangement decision contributed greatly to the show's informal, intimate vibe. Cobain turns in a memorable performance of a song that was always one of his most affecting statements about his own ailment and discontent.

From here on in, Cobain seems to grow more relaxed and confident. One of the themes of jokes during soundcheck—MTV's "superstar treatment"—winds up working well during the show too. "Aren't we, like, a rich rock band?" Cobain cracks as everyone waits for one of the Meat Puppets' guitars to be brought out. "Shouldn't we have a million guitars?"

Despite the informal, jokey vibe, Coletti recalls that the Nirvana *Unplugged* shoot was remarkably tight and hassle free. "With most *Unplugged*'s, we tend to run through the set, have a chat and then do a few songs over again. But this was truly one take—every song, straight through, in one hour. We didn't have to change tapes, which is a rarity. Usually we have to stop and put up a second load of audio and video tapes to get the last few songs. But this was really tight—something like 56 minutes from start to finish."

Cobain pulled out all the stops on the final song—a riveting version of "Where Did You Sleep Last Night," a traditional tune recorded by another of his musical heroes, the American folksinging archetype, Leadbelly. Having done pained, screaming justice to the death-haunted ballad, Cobain left the stage, never to return.

"I really tried to get him to do an encore," Alex Coletti remembers. "I had Dave, Chris and Pat ready to do it. But Kurt just wasn't into it. I was just doing my job for MTV at that point, trying to get that one extra song in the can, to see if the night could produce one more gem. The pleading went on for about five minutes. Finally Kurt said, 'I can't top that last song.' And when he said that, I backed off. 'Cause I knew he was right."

Guitar World, March 1995

Seek and Destroy

He played them. He smashed them. He had them build some more. *Guitar World* looks at Kurt Cobain's collection of custom Fenders and Ferringtons.

By Alan di Perna

IFE IS NEVER easy for a left-handed guitarist, even a successful one. They just don't make nearly as many lefty guitars as they do righties. Selection is always limited. But life is especially tough for a destructive left-handed guitarist—like Kurt Cobain. The rock ritual of smashing your guitar on stage had a special poignancy in Cobain's case. He really had to *hunt* for the things. After the phenomenal success of *Nevermind*, however, there were suddenly people who wanted to make custom guitars specially for Kurt Cobain. Two of them—luthier Danny Ferrington, and Larry L. Brooks of the Fender Custom Shop—got to do just that.

Interestingly, it was the guitar-smashing thing that led Cobain to both master builders. He hooked up with Danny Ferrington via Richard Thompson's guitar technician, who was friendly with Nirvana roadie Nick Close, who was desperately searching for left-handed necks to replace the ones Kurt had destroyed on stage. (Got all that?) "Talk to Danny Ferrington," was the advice that Close received. Which he did. The luthier helped Close track down a cache of southpaw necks and then volunteered his services as a guitar builder as well. At the time, he was compiling a book of guitars he'd built for players like Pete Townshend, Ry Cooder, David Lindley, Elvis Costello, Henry Kaiser, Albert Lee, and David Hidalgo called *Ferrington Guitars* (HarperCollins). He told Close, "I'd love to make Kurt a guitar and have it be in this book." Cobain liked the idea.

"So Kurt called me from the backstage of *Saturday Night Live*, when Nirvana was doing the show," Ferrington narrates. "We talked for a long time about what he wanted. Basically, he loved Fender Mustangs, but he also hated them because you couldn't tune them. And it's hard to raise the action. He thought you could improve on it. He essentially wanted a more sophisticated Fender Mustang. So we talked about the features he wanted. Then the band went to Australia. Kurt faxed me over a little drawing that he'd done, with the pickup placements and other little notes."

The instrument Ferrington built is depicted in his book. In body shape and headstock, it's loosely modeled on a Fender Mustang, but it has a Gibson-style Tune-O-Matic bridge and three Bartolini pickups. The bridge pickup is a humbucker, while the neck and middle pickups are single coils. The middle pickup is angled. The bridge pickup, Ferrington further explains, "has a coil tap, so you can get series, parallel, and single coil. Kurt said he wanted a lot of switch options."

The bridge pickup variations are governed by a small toggle switch located below the guitar's two knobs (a tone and a volume). There's also a Strat-style pickup selector. The instrument's body is made of basswood, with a maple neck and rosewood fretboard. The baby blue body color and tortoise-shell pickguard were Cobain's choices, as were the heart-shaped fret inlays.

"Kurt wanted the guitar set up really heavy," Ferrington recalls, "like a 0.058 low E string. Because the Mustang is a short-scale guitar you can use really heavy strings, like a jazz player might use. That combination of short scale and heavy strings was one of the keys to Kurt's signature sound."

When the instrument was finished, Cobain and his missus, Courtney Love, stopped by Ferrington's shop to collect it. "They had to be the weirdest couple in the world," the luthier says with a laugh. "She's so over the top, and he was so sensitive and soft-spoken and polite. He couldn't have been a nicer young fella. You could tell he was really talented. He'd sit there and play the guitar and he had really beautiful hands, with real long fingers. Chet Atkins has hands like that. Courtney asked him, 'Honey, are you gonna smash that guitar too?' He said, 'Oh no, this is going to be my recording guitar.' "

That was shortly before work began on *In Utero*. Not long after the album was completed, Cobain became involved with the Fender Custom Shop. Once again, Nirvana's management had initially contacted Fender in a desperate search for replacement necks and parts.

"I was able to track down what they needed," says Fender Director of Artist Relations Mark Wittenberg, "so they could keep his guitars up and running. Then we were contacted and told that Kurt had an idea for a guitar—something that he had in his mind's eye but wasn't really seeing out there in the real world. His favorite guitar was a Mustang, but there were things about the lines of the Jaguar that he really liked, too."

Wittenberg and Fender master builder Larry L. Brooks journeyed to Cobain and Love's Hollywood apartment to discuss the guitar. The couple were just in the process of moving out. Like Ferrington, the Fender guys were impressed with Cobain's courteous manner.

"He was very soft-spoken and very gentle," Brooks recalls. "As it turned out, we'd gotten him out of bed. He'd been out or played the night before, so he was still a little tired. But as we started talking about the guitar, the adrenaline started flowing. He was very easy to work with. He knew what he wanted, but at the same time he was able to say, 'You're the builder, so you know the best way to accomplish what I'm after.' He was very open minded that way."

To explain what he wanted, Cobain hit on the idea of taking Polaroids of a Mustang and a Jaguar, cutting the photos in half and gluing them together in a way that combined the upper part of the Mustang body with the lower portion of the Jag body. The resulting hybrid creature was named the "Jagstang." Brooks blew up the composite picture in an enlarger, traced the body shape and cut out a body that was sent to Cobain. The guitarist suggested some modifications to enhance the body's balance. At one point he also sent

Brooks one of his favorite necks to copy. In very short order, a prototype instrument was completed. "It took less time to design and build the guitar than it does just to communicate with some other artists," says Brooks.

The resulting instrument has an alder body, plus a 24-inch scale maple neck with a rosewood fretboard and vintage-style fretwire. At Cobain's request, Brooks used stock Mustang hardware from Japan, where the guitars are still produced. (According to Nirvana guitar tech Earnie Bailey, the bridge was later changed to a Tune-O-Matic.) The neck pickup is a single-coil Fender Texas Special, which was originally designed as a bridge pickup for Fender's Stevie Ray Vaughan model. The bridge pickup is a DiMarzio H-3 Humbucker.

"The Texas Special is a little hotter than most single coils," Brooks explains. "With a humbucker at the bridge, the Texas Special in the neck position really helped to balance things out so that there wasn't such a drastic drop in volume and output going from one pickup to the other."

"Kurt requested two guitars," says Mark Wittenberg, "one in solid blue and one in fiesta red." The blue instrument was delivered to Cobain, who used it on Nirvana's 1993 tour. "We were just finishing the fiesta red one," Wittenberg continues. "In fact, we were literally ready to deliver it when we received word of his death."

The red guitar has been earmarked for the Fender Museum which is being planned. Meanwhile, Fender is discussing plans to make the Jagstang model available to the general public.

KURT COBAIN of NIRVANA

Guitar World, October 1996

The Band Who Sold the World

The evolution of Nirvana, and how they came to record *Nevermind*–the great radio-friendly unit shifter which five years after its release remains the high water mark of the alternative rock era.

by Alan di Perna

It's hard to believe that five full years have passed since the release of Nirvana's *Nevermind* on September 24, 1991. The record is still very much in the present tense of Nineties rock sensibilities. As of this writing, *Nevermind* (DGC) has sold more than seven million copies. While the initial shock of Kurt Cobain's 1994 suicide has abated, his music and his world-weary lyrics continue to resonate deeply.

But it *has* been five years. All those 13- through 18-year-olds whose lives were changed by *Nevermind* are now immersed in the drab realities of life after high school. Ten-year-olds who bought the album when it first came out are now deep in the throes of puberty. And twentysomethings who picked up on *Nevermind* have either just passed the Big Three-O or are rapidly approaching it.

Which is to say, *Nevermind* has attained classic status. It is one of those rare albums that will accompany its original fans on their journey through life, while continuing to attract new generations of listeners. If *Nevermind* doesn't seem like an old record, it's partly because over the past five years, the rock scene has been entirely remade in its image. But the world into which *Nevermind* was born is one that a present-day rock teen would hardly recognize. Alternative rock and heavy metal were still very distinct, mutually hostile genres. Nirvana invaded both camps, converting troops from both sides to the New Flannel Army. The trio from the rugged Northwest altered the world of mainstream pop as well, knocking Michael Jackson from his perch atop the charts. In doing so, they paved the way for "alternative mainstream" success stories like Pearl Jam, Alanis Morissette, Bush, Stone Temple Pilots and Rage Against the Machine.

Like *Frampton Comes Alive* (A&M, 1975) or *Meet the Beatles* (Capitol, 1964), *Nevermind* is one of those records that gets incredibly successful in a way no one could have predicted or can ever quite explain. Its explosion into the mass culture firmament surprised Kurt Cobain, Chris Novoselic and Dave Grohl just as much as it did anyone else. "You want to know why we've taken off?" Grohl told *Circus* magazine in 1991. "We have no idea. We had no idea it would ever get this insane."

"I'm constantly feeling guilty in ways," Cobain told journalist Michael Deeds shortly after *Nevermind*'s release. "Our music, especially on this album, is so slick-sounding. A few years ago, I would have hated our band, to tell you the truth."

Nevermind represented a quantum leap for Nirvana, both musically and careerwise. Their previous album, *Bleach*, was recorded in three days and cost $606.17 to make. Their initial budget for *Nevermind* was $65,000—100 times larger than the budget for *Bleach*. They ended up spending twice that amount. And while *Bleach*, which was Nirvana's debut album, came out on the then-little-known indie label Sub Pop, *Nevermind* had the major label clout of Geffen Records behind it.

The two-year period that separates *Bleach* from *Nevermind* was a time of tremendous growth and upheaval for the band. They went on their first national and international tours. Cobain started up and broke off a relationship with Tobi Vail of the band Bikini Kill. And Nirvana went through several personnel shifts. Guitarist Jason Everman, who joined shortly after *Bleach*, exited the band nearly as quickly as he'd come aboard, once it became clear that his tastes were more hard rock/metal than his bandmates'. He later joined Soundgarden. Chad Channing, who played drums on *Bleach*, left the band. Nirvana's original drummer, Dale Crover, filled in for a seven-date West Coast tour. Dan Peters of Mudhoney played drums on a Nirvana single called "Sliver" and did one gig with them, before Dave Grohl finally settled into place as the group's permanent drummer.

The frequent personnel shifts and extensive touring seemed to have honed the band's songwriting, as such experiences often do. The process also seems to have sharpened the band's pop sensibilities, which are in far greater evidence on *Nevermind* than on the sludge-guitar heavy *Bleach*. But Nirvana biographer Michael Azerrad suggests that those same pop sensibilities existed all along, and that Cobain deliberately suppressed them on *Bleach* in an effort to conform with Sub Pop's retro Seventies metal agenda of that time.

"Half of the songs on *Nevermind* were written at the time of *Bleach*, but didn't make it onto the album," Cobain told journalist Roy Trakin. "So there really isn't an obvious change. We've always been fans of pop music."

A major milestone along the road to *Nevermind* came in April of 1990, when Nirvana began recording with producer Butch Vig at Smart Studios, his recording facility in Madison, Wisconsin. Now perhaps best known as the leader of the band Garbage, Vig was then an up-and-coming indie producer with well-regarded records by the Laughing Hyenas, Smashing Pumpkins, Firetown, Tad and Killdozer, among others, to his credit. In the week Nirvana spent at Smart, they recorded six songs that would later turn up on *Nevermind:* "In Bloom," "Dive," "Lithium," "Breed" (originally titled "Imodium"), "Stay Away" (originally titled "Pay to Play") and "Polly." They also made an unsuccessful stab at another tune, "Sappy," which they'd attempted to record at an earlier date, also with unsatisfactory results.

The Smart sessions were originally intended for release as

Nirvana's second album on Sub Pop. But a series of events led the band to change their plans. First, Chad Channing left Nirvana in May of 1990. And then the prospect of major-label interest started to become more than an idle rumor.

"We lost Chad and there was uncertainty with that," Novoselic told a radio interviewer in Australia. "We didn't want to release [the Smart sessions]. If we did anything, we wanted it to be with a new drummer. [Also] Sub Pop was doing some wheeling and dealing. They were going to sign a licensing deal with a big label and that kinda scared us. There were so many variables to consider; it wasn't wise to put out a record at all."

"Polly" is the only song on *Nevermind* that was recorded at Smart; all the other tracks were re-recorded (although the final versions are said to be very similar to those laid down at Smart). As for "Polly," the band and producer realized there was something special in Cobain's solo acoustic performance of this disquieting rape scenario, which was based on an actual newspaper account he'd read. The dramatic twist was that the very anti-violence, pro-woman Cobain sang the song from the attacker's point of view.

"Just because I say 'I' in a song doesn't necessarily mean it's me," Cobain later commented. "A lot of people have a problem with that. It's just the way I write, usually—taking on someone else's personality or character. I'd rather just use someone else's example, because, I dunno, my life is kinda boring. So I take stories from television, and things I've read and heard."

" 'Polly' was done with a really cheap acoustic five-string guitar that Kurt had," recalls Vig. "It had this plunky sound. The original strings were still on it. He never changed them, and he never tuned the guitar either. It was down about a step and a half from E."

Earlier on, Nirvana had attempted to record a full-band electric version of "Polly" for their *Blew* EP. The acoustic performance on *Nevermind* is no doubt closer in spirit to the song as it sounded when Cobain first wrote it. It also sheds light on the dynamic between Cobain as a songwriter and the rest of the group as interpreters of his material.

"It [*songwriting*] is usually done on an acoustic guitar, sitting around in my underwear, just picking out riffs, pieces of songs," Cobain said on Australian radio. "Chris and Dave have a big part in deciding on how long a song should be and how many parts it should have. So I don't like to be considered as the whole songwriter. But I do come up with the basics of it. I come up with the singing style and I write the lyrics, usually minutes before we record."

Grohl became a member of Nirvana in September of 1990, joining them from the Washington D.C. hardcore band Scream. His muscular yet agile drumming took Nirvana's power trio sound to a new plateau. Grohl's arrival also sparked a fresh burst of group songwriting. In a Tacoma, Washington, rehearsal space that they shared with a local bar band, Nirvana embarked on a regimen of daily, 15-hour band practices for a period of four or five months.

"We came up with so much stuff where we'd go, 'God, this is the best thing we've ever done!' Then we'd forget how to play it," Grohl told *Circus* magazine. "So many songs got thrown away, until we finally said, 'Maybe we should start recording them on a cassette.' So we'd record them, then lose the cassette."

Two songs that didn't get away were "Smells Like Teen Spirit" and "Come As You Are," tunes that would prove to be cornerstone tracks of *Nevermind*. The attention-grabbing title of "Teen Spirit" was born on a typically relaxed evening at the Cobain residence, as Kurt explained to Australian radio listeners:

"A friend of mine and I were goofing around my house one night. We were kinda drunk, and we were writing graffiti all over the walls of my house. And she wrote, 'Kurt smells like Teen Spirit.' Earlier on, we'd been having this discussion about teen revolution and stuff like that. And I took [what she wrote] as a compliment. I thought she was saying that I was a person who could inspire. I just thought it was a nice little title. And it turns out she just meant that I smelled like that deodorant [called Teen Spirit]. I didn't even know that deodorant existed until after the song was written."

Geffen Records had been taking an active interest in Nirvana since April of 1990, when Gary Gersh—then an A&R man for Geffen and currently head of Capitol Records—saw the band play at the Pyramid club in New York. Gersh had been brought to the show by Kim Gordon and Thurston Moore of Sonic Youth. This set in motion a chain of events that would lead to Nirvana's signing with Geffen. The deal was formally consummated on April 30, 1991. In May, the band arrived in Los Angeles to begin recording what would become *Nevermind*.

According to *Come As You Are* (Doubleday, 1994), Michael Azerrad's Nirvana bio, it was Gary Gersh's suggestion that the band re-record their six Smart session tracks for *Nevermind*. But it was Nirvana's own call to use Vig as a producer. They chose him over several bigger name producers, including Scott Litt, Don Dixon and David Briggs. Apparently, Vig's work on the Smart sessions had impressed the band.

"Butch was just easy to work with," Novoselic told Australian radio. "Laid back and really attentive to what's going on. He works hard but he doesn't work the band hard."

Butch Vig says that the band, glad to be in sunny Los Angeles, was generally in good spirits for the *Nevermind* sessions. "Kurt was enjoying himself when we made that record. That was before they got really big, and they had kind of a casual attitude toward making the record. There wasn't a lot of pressure—I felt more pressure making that record than they did, because it was really the first major label record I had made."

With an initial budget of $65,000, the band could certainly take a more leisurely approach than they'd taken with *Bleach*. They began with three days of pre-production, running down the tunes with Vig in a North Hollywood rehearsal hall. One of the first things Vig noticed is the huge impact Grohl's arrival had made on the band's sound.

"Kurt had called me up and said, 'I've got the best drummer in the world!' I thought, 'Yeah, right. I've heard that one before.' But the first time we went in that rehearsal space and started running through the songs, it was just amazing. Dave was incredibly powerful and dead on the groove. I could tell from the way Kurt and Chris were playing with him that they had definitely kicked their music up another notch, in terms of intensity."

The pre-production chores were fairly light work; Nirvana had already recorded half the material with Vig once before. And they were well-rehearsed on most of the newer tunes. "Frankly, I didn't want to beat the songs into the ground," says Vig. "I just wanted to hear the arrangements and maybe tighten things up a little bit."

Vig had already heard a rough rehearsal cassette of "Teen Spirit" but he was knocked out the first time he heard Nirvana play it live in the rehearsal room. "I kept having them play it over and over again, because it was so fucking good! I was literally pacing around the room, saying to myself, 'This is amazing!' There wasn't much that needed to be done with the song. I think we did a little arranging. At the end of each chorus, there's a little ad lib thing Kurt did with the guitar. Originally that only happened at the end of the song; he did it a whole bunch of times. I suggested moving that up into each chorus and cutting the choruses down a little bit. Just some minor tweaking of the arrangements."

From there, the band moved over to Sound City Studios in nearby Van Nuys. A funky old place in a poor, largely Hispanic part of the San Fernando Valley, Sound City has a good classic rock and metal track record (Fleetwood Mac, Foreigner, Petty, Dio, Crazy Horse, Ratt). Most important, the studio has what Vig and the band felt they needed in order to get the primal rock sound they were after: a large recording room and a vintage Neve console. "At that point, I'd never done any work in Los Angeles," says Vig. "But I knew that was where the band wanted to work, and I knew of Sound City's reputation. I worked out a deal so it was cost-effective for us to go there. It was sight unseen. We just booked it and went in."

On a typical day, says Vig, "we'd be in the studio by around noon or one and we'd leave around midnight or one in the morning." The band set up in Sound City's large room, Studio A, to record basic tracks. "When we cut basics, it went pretty fast," Vig recalls. "I think it took five or six days in all. Dave was set up in the middle of the room. We built a big drum tunnel on the front of his bass drum, so we could mike it from a distance and still isolate it from all the bleed in the rest of the room. Chris had his SVT bass rig off to the side, but he could play in the room. His headphones were set up next to the drums. Kurt's amps were in a little isolation area, but he was also in the room and he could sing into a mic. We'd start running a song down and they'd usually get the basic track in two or three takes. If there was a missed chord or a bad bass note, we'd go back and punch in [the correct notes] right away.

" 'Territorial Pissings' was basically a first take. 'Lithium' was a little harder. That was the only track we used a click track on at the start of the song. Because, for whatever reason, the band kept speeding up really fast. We decided that we wanted to keep it at a real even tempo. Dave had never played with a click track before, but it was not a problem for him at all. After three or four takes with the click, we nailed it.

"After the first couple of takes of 'Territorial Pissings,' that's when they did that song, 'Endless Nameless' [*the surprise noise track that kicks in 13 minutes and 51 seconds after the end of the album's ostensible final song, 'Something in the Way'*]. Kurt got really frustrated because the song kept speeding up and they were just not playing particularly tight. And he launched into that bonus track on the CD and just totally went off. In the middle of the song, he smashed his guitar to bits. So we spent the better part of the rest of that day driving around Los Angeles trying to find a left-handed replacement guitar."

Another problematic track was "Something in the Way." "They originally wanted to cut it as a full-on band," Vig explains. "But that proved difficult to record. It just was not happening. Kurt was not very happy. Finally he came over to me and said, 'It needs to sound like this...' And he picked up his old five-string acoustic guitar [*the same one used on 'Polly'*]. He sat on the couch in the control room and started to sing and play."

Realizing he was on to what could be a master take, Vig quickly set up some microphones. "I turned off the air conditioner and everything else and had the phones shut off. He was playing and singing so quietly. But we got it down on tape. Later on, we overdubbed drums and Kurt added some harmonies. But it was all built around the acoustic track."

Vig remembers Cobain as someone who was generally willing to let others share in his creative processes. "He was pretty open to all sorts of ideas. He had different lyrics he would bring in and show me. And he'd say, 'I got a couple of melodies here. Which one do you like better?' And he'd sing the song in a couple of different versions and I'd give him some feedback on it."

After basic tracks were completed, Nirvana moved over to Sound City's other, smaller room, Studio B, for overdubs. "We started adding the second rhythm guitar to songs," says Vig, "and Kurt started working some more on his vocals. Dave did some harmonies."

Lead vocal sessions were generally done in a one-on-one setting, with just Cobain and the producer present. The vocal mic was set up in the main studio area, "but it was basically like a lounge area," says Vig. "There were candles in there, and a big rug on the floor. A pretty cool vibe. Dave and Chris were around, but they'd be off playing pool or watching TV. They'd pop in to the control room and listen every now and then, but Kurt kind of wanted to be left alone when he was doing his vocals. He also didn't really like to use headphones when he sang, so we set up a fairly elaborate system where he could use speakers."

Cobain's legendary impatience with multiple takes came to the fore at this time. "He really wanted to do everything on the first or second take," says Vig. "He'd do a couple of takes and say, 'That's it. I'm not gonna do it anymore.' The tricky part was trying to figure out how to motivate him to give really good performances. Sometimes his first or second takes were brilliant, but sometimes they needed work. They needed to be more focused. What I ended up doing was recording everything he sang, even the warmups. A lot of times, I'd actually be going for a first take, but he would think it was just a warmup. Then I'd have the engineer flip to a new track and I'd tell Kurt, 'Okay, you're ready for your first take.' If I was lucky, I could get as many as four takes out of him. Then I'd take the best pieces of each one and make a master out of it."

Cobain's painful, undiagnosable stomach condition would sometimes bring sessions to a halt, Vig remembers. "He was very sensitive to certain foods. Sometimes we'd eat dinner and he'd get sick half an hour later and end up spending 45 minutes in the bathroom. He was constantly taking Pepto Bismol and things to relieve some of his pain."

But for all that, the mood in the studio was generally upbeat. "Kurt and Chris were really happy that Dave had joined the band," says Vig. "They were in L.A., they'd just signed a record deal with Geffen, they had a bit of cash, so they'd go out and do a little partying. I know they used to go down to Venice and stay up all night. After we'd finish working in the studio at midnight or one, they'd go and stay out 'til the sun came up. So sometimes I'd get to the studio at one and they wouldn't show up 'til three because they'd slept in. But basically, they showed up when they needed to show up. There wasn't any real serious partying going on in the studio. They were there to work.

While in L.A., the band stayed at the Oakwood Apartments in nearby Universal City. "A couple of times I went to pick them up there and they had definitely turned their place into a bachelor pad. There were cans of food lying open everywhere and clothes thrown all over the place and acoustic guitars lying around the room. I know they were getting a big kick out of staying there because the band Europe was staying next to them. That was the band that had a big hit in the Eighties with 'The Final Countdown.' The guys in Europe would all go sit out with their girlfriends by the pool everyday. And I remember Chris and Dave and Kurt making fun of them. They were not big Europe fans."

Working at Sound City at the same time as Nirvana were the Sidewinders, an Arizona band that Vig had recorded who were now working with David Briggs (who, embarrassingly enough, Nirvana had rejected as a producer for *Nevermind*). Vig recalls that the guys in the Sidewinders "kept coming by and asking, 'Wow, can you play us some stuff that Nirvana's doing?' That was the first sense I got that there were people out there who were really totally obsessed with Nirvana."

The band reached the end of the 16 days they'd booked at Sound

City before they'd finished overdubbing. They booked an additional four or five days at Devonshire Studios in nearby Burbank, where they completed their overdubs and did some preliminary mixing. One of the very last overdubs to be completed was the cello part on "Something in the Way," the track that had given them difficulties all along. The cello part was played by Kirk Panning.

"That song really wasn't even written until a week before we went into the studio," Cobain told Australian radio. "I knew I wanted cello on it, but after all the music was recorded for it, we'd kinda forgotten about putting a cello on. We had one more day in the studio and we decided, 'Oh geez, we should hire a cellist, you know, and put something in.' We were at a party and were asking some of our friends if they knew anyone who could play cello, and it just happened that one of our best friends in L.A. is a cellist. So we took him into the studio on the last day and said, 'Here, play something.' And he came up with a part right away. It just fell in like dominoes."

From a technical standpoint, however, it wasn't all *that* easy. "Kirk is a good cello player," says Vig, "but we had a hard time getting his instrument in tune with Kurt's guitar. That old five-string acoustic of Kurt's was tuned down a few steps and wasn't really tuned to any standard pitch. I remember I fretted over the whole track. It was tricky getting Chris' bass in tune with the guitar, too. You couldn't use any kind of a standard tuner."

While at Devonshire, Vig and the band also took a first stab at mixing the record. "I mixed three or four tracks with the band," says the producer, "but none of us were very happy with how they came out. To me, they sounded too rough. Kurt would say, 'Take all the high end off the guitars.' And I would say, 'I don't want them to sound muddy.' There was also a tendency to bury the vocals more. The mixes sounded more punk rock that way, but the songs didn't sound as focused to me."

So they decided to call in someone else to mix the album. Geffen's Gary Gersh sent over a list of possible names. "Scott Litt was on top of the list," Vig recalls, "but Kurt said, 'No, I don't want to sound like R.E.M.' Ed Stasium was also on the list. To which Kurt said,

'No, I don't want to sound like the Smithereens.' He went all the way to the bottom of the list and Andy Wallace was there. It said 'Slayer' next to his name. And Kurt said, 'Get this guy.' "

The mixes were done at Scream, another San Fernando Valley studio. "Basically, I'd let Andy go over the tracks by himself for a few hours," Vig recalls. "When he got everything up, he'd call me in, and I'd bring in the band and we would nit-pick stuff. Basically, we mixed a song or two a day. The whole record took nine or 10 days to mix."

Despite the fact that Wallace was Cobain's own choice, and that the band participated in the mixing process, Cobain would later complain to the press that Wallace's mixes made *Nevermind* sound too slick, and that it was "closer to Mötley Crüe than a punk rock record."

"But I think part of that was just Kurt's reaction to having *Nevermind* be so successful," Vig speculates. "If it had only sold 50,000 copies, he probably wouldn't have had any comments on whether it was too slick or not slick enough."

By the time the finished masters were handed to the label, the band had spent $130,000 which, despite being twice their initial budget, is still a relatively small amount for a multi-platinum album. With the music out of the way, attention turned to the cover art.

"One day Dave and I were sitting around watching a documentary on babies being born under water," said Cobain in his Australian radio interview. "I thought that was a really neat image, so we decided, 'Let's put that on the album cover.' Then when we got back a picture of a baby underwater, I thought it would look nice [to add] a fish hook with a dollar bill on it. And so an image was born."

The back cover of *Nevermind* features a photograph by Cobain taken some years earlier, with a background comprising a collage he made from photos of raw meat, vaginas (according to some accounts) and figures from a painting of Dante's *Inferno*. In the foreground is Chim Chim, his toy monkey who'd appeared in earlier Nirvana artwork.

"I was in a bohemian photography stage, you know?" Cobain

later said. "If you look real close, there's also a picture of Kiss, in the back, standing on a slab of beef."

Nevermind was released on September 24, 1991. Like all rock albums, it documents the artists' world at the time the record was made. This momentous recording happened to catch Nirvana at a high point: in the midst of a creative groundswell, somewhere between obscurity and superstardom. "We're experiencing the typical independent-band-going-onto-a-major-label-punk-rock-crisis," Cobain said in 1991, shortly after *Nevermind* was released. But he also acknowledged the existence of something more important than passing musical fashions and fickle perceptions of "credibility" and "authenticity." On a level beyond all that, he appeared to realize that the songs on *Nevermind* could stand the test of time.

"People have opened up to an appreciation of hard rock in punk, and it's great that they've fused together," Cobain told *Monday Morning Replay* in December 1991. "Now it's time to appreciate the pop side. Attitude is one thing. But a good song is the most important thing. It's the only way to really touch someone."

KURT COBAIN of NIRVANA

Guitar World, August 1997

Super Fuzz Big Muff

The definitive guide to Kurt Cobain's grungy assortment of pawn shop prizes, turbo-charged stomp boxes and blown woofers.

By Chris Gill

URT COBAIN NEVER intended to become a guitar hero. Although he certainly loved to play guitar, he viewed his playing as the lesser part of a greater musical equation. The irony is that Cobain became one of the most widely emulated guitarists of the Nineties. Before the release of Nirvana's breakthrough album, *Nevermind*, aspiring rock guitarists spent hours daily studying music theory and practicing finger exercises. After *Nevermind*, they devoted their time to searching pawn shops for the perfect Seventies fuzz box. Suddenly it became fashionable to mock technique, and the phrase "I just play from the heart" was on the lips of every guitarist from Seattle to CBGB's.

Cobain was much aware of the revolution he'd started. "I can't play like Segovia," he told Fender's *Frontline* magazine. "The flip side of that is that Segovia could probably never have played like me." While Cobain acknowledged that his playing technique was limited, he reminded guitarists that a few simple chords played with honest emotion can speak volumes—in Cobain's case, volumes that could make ears bleed.

Cobain must have been amused when magazines like *Guitar World* and *Guitar Player* requested interviews and when Fender approached him to design a guitar. But here's where another irony exists—although Cobain often said that he didn't care very much about equipment, he certainly possessed more than a passing interest in the tools of his trade. Cobain may not have collected vintage Gibsons, Martins, D'Angelicos and what-not, but he owned an eccentric cache of budget models, low-end imports and pawn shop prizes—most pursued with the same passion as a Gibson collector seeking a mint '59 Les Paul. Even when he could afford the best, Cobain's taste in instruments never changed. "Junk is always best," Cobain stated matter-of-factly to Jeff Gilbert in a February 1992 *Guitar World* interview. "I use whatever I can find at junk shops."

As increasing numbers of aspiring musicians made Cobain their mentor, they began to wonder how he created the wide array of sometimes angry, sometimes ethereal tones that poured from his battered guitars and over-powered amps. The uninitiated speculated that Cobain used special processors and studio trickery to obtain his sound. As Cobain's influence spread across the world, so did the rumors about what he played.

Guitar World feels that the time has come for the truth about Cobain's equipment to be revealed. To solve these mysteries and dispel the rumors, we contacted the most reliable sources available—the dealers who sold him his equipment, the engineers and producers who worked with him in the studio, and the technicians who looked after his gear on the road. A couple of well-researched web sites on the Internet, Chris Lawrence's site (www.geocities.com/SunsetStrip/Towers/5890/kurtseq.html) and Brian Haberman's site (members.aol.com/bhabes/private/nkcequi.htm), also supplied many useful details. Michael Azerrad's *Come As You Are—The Story of Nirvana* (Main Street/Doubleday) provided excellent background information and photographs, and we also pored over the few interviews on the subject granted by Cobain himself.

Cobain probably would have laughed at the idea of a magazine scrutinizing the minute details of his gear. "I've never considered musical equipment very sacred," he once said. But for the thousands of guitarists who consider Cobain's music sacred, it's important to understand what he played and why he played it.

SCENTLESS APPRENTICE—
COBAIN'S VIRGIN MUSICAL YEARS

Kurt Donald Cobain was born in Aberdeen, Washington, on February 20, 1967. Growing up in the company of several musicians—his Uncle Chuck played in a rock band and his Aunt Mary played guitar—Cobain showed an early interest in music. As a youngster, he would often bang at the strings on a plastic toy guitar while singing along with his favorite Beatles records. Cobain's Aunt Mary encouraged his musical development and attempted to teach him guitar when he was seven, but he had difficulty learning.

Expressing desires of becoming "John Lennon playing drums" when he grew up, Cobain started taking drum lessons in the third grade. He switched to guitar in 1981 when his Uncle Chuck gave him a used electric guitar and a small 10-watt amp for his 14th birthday. "As soon as I got my guitar, I just became so obsessed with it," Cobain told Michael Azerrad. "I don't think it was even a Harmony. I think it was a Sears." Cobain took guitar lessons for less than a month—just long enough to learn how to play AC/DC's "Back in Black." Those three chords served him well when he began writing his own songs shortly thereafter.

Cobain soon set his sights on forming a band. One day, a couple of friends invited him to jam in an abandoned meat locker that they used as a practice space. Afterwards, Cobain foolishly left his guitar in the locker and was subsequently unable to return and get it back. When he finally made it back to the rehearsal space a few months later, he found his guitar in pieces. He salvaged the neck, hardware, and electronics and made a new body for the guitar in wood shop. But Cobain lacked the skills to make the restored instrument intonate properly. Later he acquired a replacement, but details about that guitar are unknown.

When Cobain was 17, his mother married Pat O'Connor, whose ensuing infidelity led to a situation that greatly facilitated Cobain's acquisition of musical gear. After Cobain's mother learned that Pat was cheating on her, she dumped his rifle and gun collection in the river. Cobain observed his mother's antics and later encouraged some of the neighborhood kids to fish his stepdad's weapons out of the river. Cobain sold the guns and used the proceeds to buy a used Peavey Vintage amplifier with two 12-inch speakers. Once the Peavey became a member of the Cobain household, Aberdeen rarely knew a peaceful evening.

In early 1985 Cobain moved in with his natural father who discouraged his son's musical pursuits and convinced him to pawn his guitar. After about a week, Cobain got his guitar out of hock and moved out. He almost lost the guitar again when he loaned it to a drug dealer, but managed to repossess it a few months later. With this unknown guitar and the Peavey amp in hand, Cobain formed his first band, Fecal Matter, in late 1985.

The Peavey amp disappeared sometime between early 1986 and late 1987. Krist Novoselic remembers that Cobain gave the amp to him for about a week, in what apparently was a friendly attempt to get him to join Fecal Matter. Novoselic declined on both offers. The amp disappeared sometime after that.

By late 1987 Novoselic finally agreed to form a band with Cobain and drummer Aaron Burckhard, which they called Skid Row (no relation to the Sebastian Bach-fronted metal outfit of the same name). Photos from this era show Cobain playing a right-hand model sunburst Univox Hi-Flyer flipped over and strung for left-handed playing. According to Azerrad, Cobain's amp during this period was a tiny Fender Champ. Also around this time, Cobain acquired a Univox Superfuzz but it was stolen from his rehearsal space.

The band's name changed frequently, from Fecal Matter to such similarly choice monikers as Ted Ed Fred, Pen Cap Chew, Throat Oyster, Windowpane and Bliss. Eventually they settled on Nirvana. When Burckhard proved too unreliable, Cobain and Novoselic kicked him out of the band and enlisted drummer Dale Crover, whom they temporarily stole from the Melvins. Three weeks later, on January 23, 1988, Nirvana recorded its first studio demo at Reciprocal Studio with Jack Endino—whose early production/engineering/mixing credits include Soundgarden, Green River, Tad and Mudhoney—behind the board.

BLOND AMBITION–THE BLEACH YEARS

Jack Endino was not supposed to work on Nirvana's demo session, but because he was impressed by Crover's playing with the Melvins, he insisted on doing the recording. The band's working relationship with Endino proved to be exceptionally fortuitous. A few months after working with Nirvana for the first time, Endino played the band's demo tape for Jonathan Poneman of Sub Pop Records, who signed the band to the label. Three of the songs that Nirvana recorded during that session ended up on *Bleach*, the band's first album.

"They didn't have a whole lot of equipment," says Endino. "In the early days, Kurt used a Randall amplifier head. It may not have even been a tube model—I think it was solid-state. I don't recall what the speakers were."

The band liked working with Endino, and they returned to Reciprocal Studios several times during the year to record more songs, although Chad Channing replaced Crover on drums. Nirvana signed a contract with Sub Pop, and in late December 1988, they entered Reciprocal Studios to record *Bleach*. The album was recorded in three days at a cost of $606.16, although five tracks from earlier sessions were included on the final album. Most of the remaining songs from the various Reciprocal sessions were released several years later on *Incesticide*.

"When they recorded *Bleach*, the Randall was in the shop, so they borrowed my amp, which was a Sixties Fender Twin," Endino recalls. "I'm a tube nut, so everything was tweaked and up to spec on that amp, but it didn't have speakers because I had fried them. Kurt brought in a little closed-back 2x12 cabinet with two Celestions, most likely 70-watt models. He was using a little orange Boss DS-1 distortion pedal and these Univox guitars [Hi-Flyers] that looked like Mosrites. The pickups were stock. I ended up getting one of those pickups from him once, because he was smashing those guitars all the time. I said, 'You must have some extra pickups,' and he said,

'Oh yeah. Here's one.' It was in two pieces. I was able to stick the wires together and use it. It's not the greatest sounding pickup in the world, but it seemed to work for him."

While playing at a Halloween party on October 30, 1988, in a dormitory at Washington's Evergreen State College, Cobain smashed a guitar—a sunburst Univox Hi-Flyer—for the first time. According to Cobain, his destructive habit started due to his frustration with Channing's drumming. "I got so pissed off at Chad that I'd jump into the drum set, then smash my guitar," Cobain told Azerrad. "That really is how the instrument smashing came about."

In 1989 Nirvana went on its first American tour. According to Earnie Bailey, a Seattle guitar repairman who was friends with Novoselic and who often worked as a technician for the band, Cobain's live rig during this period was a red Epiphone ET270, a solid-state Randall amp head, a BFI Bullfrog 4x12 cabinet and a Boss DS-1 distortion. When his guitar was destroyed beyond repair, Cobain would look for cheap replacements in pawn shops or have Sub Pop ship him guitars via Federal Express. Sometimes, fans would sell Cobain a guitar, which he would later destroy with extreme gusto.

"I heard stories about Kurt's guitar destruction from the Sub Pop people early on," says Endino. "When he was out on the road he'd call them up and say, 'I don't know what got into me, but I just smashed up my guitar.' I don't think he was planning on smashing guitars from day one. It was just something he did. The poor Sub Pop people would call all the pawn shops up and down the coast, looking for Univox guitars."

Between tours, Cobain often bought equipment from Guitar Maniacs in Tacoma, Washington, and Danny's Music in Everett, Washington. According to Rick King, owner of Guitar Maniacs, Cobain "bought a whole bunch of Univox Hi-Flyers—both the P-90 version and ones with humbuckers. Those pickups have huge output and are completely over the top. He broke a lot of those guitars. We sold him several of them for an average of $100 each over the course of five years."

Although humbucker-equipped Univox Hi-Flyers apparently were

Cobain's favorite guitars in the pre-*Nevermind* days, he often appeared on stage with other models, including a blue Gibson SG and a sunburst left-handed Greco Mustang copy that he bought from Guitar Maniacs. The Mustang copy allegedly was destroyed on July 9, 1989, at a gig in Pennsylvania, but it may have experienced some form of reincarnation since a similar guitar is seen in photos of Nirvana at a gig at Seattle's HUB East Ballroom on January 6, 1990.

Cobain purchased what probably was his first acoustic guitar, a Stella 12-string, for $31.21 on October 12, 1989. He brought the Stella to Smart Studios in Wisconsin to record some demos with Butch Vig in April 1990. The guitar wasn't exactly a studio musician's dream. "It barely stays in tune," Cobain told Jeff Gilbert in a February 1992 *Guitar World* interview. "I have to use duct tape to hold the tuning keys in place." At some point in the Stella's history, the steel strings had been replaced with six nylon strings, only five of which were intact during the session. However, the guitar sounded good enough to Vig, who recorded Cobain playing a solo acoustic version of "Polly" on that guitar. That track can be heard on *Nevermind*.

Cobain didn't seem to be exceptionally particular about what equipment he was playing through. Perhaps the best example of this was when Nirvana cut the "Sliver" single. "I was in the studio working on a record with Tad," says Jack Endino. "Nirvana wanted to come in and record the song during Tad's dinner break, so they just used Tad's equipment." Anyone familiar with Tad's eating habits knows that Nirvana probably could have recorded an entire album during that break.

The one thing that Cobain was particular about was his effects pedals. Sometime in 1990 he bought an Electro-Harmonix Small Clone from Guitar Maniacs, and it remained a favorite and essential part of his setup to the end of his life. On January 1, 1991, Cobain used the Small Clone to record "Aneurysm," which later was issued as the b-side to the "Smells Like Teen Spirit" single.

BREEDING GROUND—
THE RECORDING OF *NEVERMIND*

Prior to formally signing with Geffen Records on April 30, 1991,

Nirvana received a $287,000 advance for the recording of *Nevermind*. The advance was somewhat meager, but it gave the band some freedom in choosing equipment. However, Cobain didn't exactly go wild with his spending.

"I sold Kurt a bunch of guitars and effects for the *Nevermind* album," says Rick King. "When they got signed to Geffen and started getting money, Kurt was still very frugal. He bought some Japanese left-handed Strats and had humbuckers installed in the Strats' lead position. He didn't spend very much money on guitars."

Apparently, Cobain developed a taste for Fender guitars just prior to recording *Nevermind*. "I like guitars in the Fender style because they have skinny necks," said Cobain in a late 1991 interview. "I've resorted to Japanese-made Fender Stratocasters because they're the most available left-handed guitars." During this period, he also acquired a left-handed '65 Jaguar that had a DiMarzio Super Distortion humbucker in the bridge position and a DiMarzio PAF in the neck position in place of the guitar's stock single-coil pickups. These modifications were made before Cobain purchased the guitar. Cobain also bought a left-handed, Lake Placid Blue '69 Fender Competition Mustang around then.

"Out of all the guitars in the whole world, the Fender Mustang is my favorite," Cobain told *GW*. "They're cheap and totally inefficient, and they sound like crap and are very small. They also don't stay in tune, and when you want to raise the string action on the fretboard, you have to loosen all the strings and completely remove the bridge. You have to turn these little screws with your fingers and hope that you've estimated it right. If you screw up, you have to repeat the process over and over until you get it right. Whoever invented that guitar was a dork. I guess I'm calling Leo Fender, the dead guy, a dork." To overcome these tuning problems, Cobain had his '69 Mustang fitted with a Gotoh Tune-O-Matic bridge, a modification that was routinely performed on the Mustangs he subsequently acquired.

Some claim that Cobain's preference for low-end guitars was a punk statement, but he insisted that it was a matter of necessity. "I don't favor them," Cobain told *Guitar World* in '92. "I can afford them. I'm left-handed and it's not very easy to find reasonably priced, high-quality left-handed guitars."

Before entering the studio, Cobain purchased a rack rig consisting of a Mesa/Boogie Studio preamp, a Crown power amp and a variety of Marshall 4x12 cabinets. "I can never find an amp that's powerful enough," Cobain told *GW*. "And I don't want to deal with hauling 10 Marshall heads. I'm lazy—I like to have it all in one package. For a preamp I have a Mesa/Boogie, and I turn all the midrange up." Cobain brought this rig along with his Mustang, Jaguar, a Japanese Strat and his Boss DS-1 and Electro-Harmonix Small Clone pedals to Sound City Studios in Van Nuys, California, where the band recorded *Nevermind* with Butch Vig.

"Kurt had a Mesa/Boogie, but we also used a Fender Bassman a lot and a Vox AC30 on *Nevermind*," Vig recalls. "I prefer getting the amp to sound distorted instead of using special effects or pedals, which lose body and the fullness of the bottom end, even though you can get nice distortion with some of them. If you get a good-sounding amp, that's 90 percent of it."

But even though Vig wasn't the biggest fan of effects pedals, he allowed Cobain to use a few on the album, especially since the guitarist felt that the DS-1 was the main factor in his tone. Cobain also used the Small Clone liberally. "That's making the watery guitar sound you hear on the pre-chorus build-up of 'Smells Like Teen Spirit' and also 'Come As You Are,' " says Vig. "We used an Electro-Harmonix Big Muff fuzz box through a Fender Bassman on 'Lithium' to get that thumpier, darker sound."

Cobain's pawn shop Stella, which he had played at the sessions held at Vig's Smart Studios a year earlier, was used again for "Something in the Way." Vig recorded the performance while Cobain sat on a couch in the control room.

Against Vig's wishes, Cobain plugged his guitar direct into the board for "Territorial Pissings." During the recording of "Lithium," Cobain instigated the noise jam that became the "hidden" track "Endless, Nameless." (This track does not appear on the first 50,000 copies of the CD.) Toward the end of the track, Cobain can be heard smashing his Japanese Stratocaster.

LOUNGE ACT—THE *NEVERMIND* TOUR

After Nirvana finished basic tracking, they opened for Dinosaur Jr on brief tours in the U.S. and Europe. The *Nevermind* tour started in Toronto on September 20, 1991, a few days before the album was released. Nick Close, Cobain's guitar tech from September 1991 until March 1992, recalls that Cobain's rig was basically the same as the one used to record *Nevermind*—the Mesa/Boogie Studio preamp, a Crown power amp, a Boss DS-1 and the Small Clone. Initially, only a handful of guitars were taken along on tour—the '65 Jaguar, the '69 Mustang and a left-handed Japanese Strat. Later, Cobain picked up a sunburst Telecaster, which he painted sky blue, then scratched off some of the paint in the shape of a heart and the word "Courtney."

"When I was working for them, the money hadn't started coming in," says Close. "There was a lot of equipment out there that would have made Kurt a lot happier on stage, but they didn't get tried because of time and money. And Kurt wasn't much of a gearhead. He didn't want to sit down and talk about what could be done."

Close says that the Crown power amp was a particular source of frustration. "It never worked very well for us," he says. "The output on that Studio preamp was very hot. Because of that, the Crown would blow up a lot, and I was always having to get it repaired." Frustrated with the Crown, Close eventually ordered two Crest 4801 power amps. Finally they had found an amp that could withstand the onslaught of abuse. Earnie Bailey referred to the Crest as "the amp that wouldn't die," and both remained in Cobain's rig until the end.

Due to the constant thrashing endured by the equipment, Close was constantly looking for replacements. "Everybody had the exact number of things needed to make the show happen," says Close. "If anything broke, we were screwed. I was trying to move them in the direction of having extra cords and pedals. Kurt started out with the Boss DS-1, and I was always looking for a backup. One time the

Crown amp blew up and took the speakers with it. We were in a music store to buy some Marshall cabinets, and I saw a DS-2 there and bought it. Kurt didn't seem to be too happy with it at first, but he put it in his rig after he broke his DS-1 in Hawaii." [*A performance photo on the insert of* In Utero *clearly shows Cobain's DS-2 and Small Clone.*]

Kurt's guitars constantly needed repairs as well. Generally, the Strat received most of the abuse. "Lately I've been using a Strat live because I don't want to ruin my Mustang yet," Cobain told *GW*. "I like to use Japanese Strats because they're a bit cheaper, and the frets are smaller than the American version's."

Close acquired a small stash of replacement necks from Fender, but soon he was replacing necks on the Strat every night. Frustrated, he visited luthier Danny Ferrington when the band arrived in Los Angeles in late December, and asked him to build some replacement necks for Cobain's guitars. Instead, Ferrington offered to build a guitar for Cobain. "Danny was in the middle of doing his book [Ferrington Guitars, *Harper Collins*], and he took the whole project and ran with it," says Close. "I was in awe of Ferrington. I don't know whether Kurt cared if someone was making him a guitar, but he seemed to read my enthusiasm."

Cobain drew a picture of what he wanted and faxed it to Ferrington from Melbourne, Australia. Ferrington delivered the finished guitar, essentially a left-handed Mustang with a Tune-O-Matic bridge, heart-shaped fingerboard inlays, a Strat-style angled output jack, and a humbucker and two single-coil Bartolini pickups, to Cobain in the summer of '92. Perhaps the most expensive guitar that Cobain ever owned, the Ferrington didn't see much action on the road and eventually was kept at home.

When money started coming in, Cobain bought more guitars, but he retained his taste for low-budget gear. Perhaps Cobain's most "extravagant" purchase during this time was a mid-Sixties Fender Electric XII, with which he wrote "Serve the Servants." This guitar was subsequently damaged when some sewage backed up into the bathtub where Kurt had it stored. Cobain allegedly left the guitar in the tub to fool potential burglars. He also returned to Guitar Maniacs, where he bought an Electro-Harmonix Echo Flanger for $99. This pedal later played a significant role in the recording of *In Utero*.

NO APOLOGIES—COBAIN RECLAIMS HIS PUNK ROOTS ON *IN UTERO*

In late February 1993, Cobain, Novoselic and Grohl traveled to Pachyderm Studios in Minnesota to record *In Utero* with Steve Albini. This time, however, Cobain left his live rig behind at home.

"For *In Utero*, Kurt primarily used his Jaguar and a Twin Reverb," Earnie Bailey said in the March 1995 issue of *Guitar World*. "Effects consisted of a Boss DS-2 distortion, a Small Clone and an Electro-Harmonix Poly Chorus." Bailey loaned the Poly Chorus to Cobain because his Echo Flanger was acting up. (The Echo Flanger, Poly Chorus and Poly Flanger all have the same circuitry but slightly different cosmetics.) The Twin Reverb was a 1982 135-watt blackface model that Cobain picked up sometime before the sessions started. Originally, it had only two of its four 6L6 output tubes in place, so it was running at half power. Cobain really liked the sound that way and told Bailey to leave the amp alone. As a prank, Bailey placed four matched tubes in the amp prior to rehearsals for *In Utero*. Cobain noticed the difference immediately, remarking that the amp sounded better than ever.

Cobain also brought along his trusty Stella acoustic, which had been equipped with new tuners and strings courtesy of Bailey. The Stella was used on three songs—"Dumb," "Pennyroyal Tea" and "All Apologies." Bailey also recalls sending a sunburst lefty Ibanez Les Paul Custom copy to the studio, but he's not certain whether the guitar was used or not.

Some of the most impressive sounds on *In Utero* were created with the Echo Flanger. Cobain dialed in a variety of effects on the unit, including the abrasive flanging effect on "Scentless Apprentice," the bizarre, wobbling vibrato sounds on "Radio Friendly Unit Shifter" and the deep chorus tones on "Heart Shaped Box."

In typical indie-rock fashion, the basic tracks for *In Utero* were completed in two weeks. The total cost of recording was $124,000—$24,000 for studio bills and $100,000 for Albini.

In February 1993, right before *In Utero* was recorded, Cobain collaborated with Fender on the design of what later became known as the Jag-Stang. According to Mark Wittenberg, who was director of artist relations for Fender until he died of a brain aneurysm on February 14, 1995, "We were contacted and told that Kurt had an idea for a guitar. His favorite guitar was a Mustang, but there were things about the lines of the Jaguar that he really liked, too." Wittenberg and builder Larry Brooks met Cobain at his apartment in Hollywood, where they discussed his plans for a guitar that combined the aesthetics of a Jaguar and a Mustang, hence the name "Jag-Stang."

The guitar Cobain envisioned featured a Mustang's neck and upper bout and a Jaguar's lower bout. He later sent Fender an illustration and specified a small, pre-CBS style headstock, double-coil Duncan Hot Rail bridge pickup, a Mustang single-coil neck pickup, and several suggestions for the body shape. Cobain also sent Fender the neck of his favorite Mustang for them to copy. A couple of different versions of the body were sent to Cobain for his approval, and once Fender came up with a shape he liked, the prototype was completed.

The prototype had a large, CBS-style headstock, a DiMarzio H-3 bridge humbucker, a Fender Texas Special neck single-coil, and stock Mustang hardware. According to Jim Vincent, Cobain's guitar tech on the *In Utero* tour, "Kurt wasn't really all that happy when he got the first Jag-Stang. He liked his Mustangs much better, even the new ones. For the month he had it, he hated it and wouldn't play it because there was no contour—it's as thick as a Tele—and it was kind of misbalanced. It was really tough to set up. Earnie immediately swapped out the pickups. Right when we got it, he routed it out and put a Duncan JB humbucker in the bridge." Bailey also installed a Tune-O-Matic bridge on the guitar. Eventually, Cobain grew comfortable enough with the Jag-Stang to use it on rare occasions for an entire show.

FROM THE CRADLE TO THE GRAVE—
THE *IN UTERO* TOUR AND THE FINAL DAYS

In Utero was released September 21, 1993, almost exactly two years after *Nevermind*. Nirvana had performed only a handful of live shows during 1993, but in October of that year the band set out on its biggest tour ever. By now Nirvana was headlining arena shows and playing to increasingly larger audiences. However, Cobain's stage rig remained almost the same as before, probably because it was so excruciatingly loud. The only changes were the addition of the Electro-Harmonix Echo Flanger (which alternated duty with Bailey's Poly Chorus) and a Tech 21 SansAmp. (A good live photo showing all of Kurt's pedals is on the cover of *From the Muddy Banks of the Wishkah*.) "His signal chain went as follows: guitar-Boss DS-2-SansAmp-Poly Chorus or Echo Flanger (whichever worked that day)-Small Clone-amp," says Bailey.

According to Vincent, the SansAmp was the main source of Cobain's distorted tone. "He also used the DS-2, but that was mainly used on the acoustic guitar for 'The Man Who Sold the World,' " says Vincent. "Occasionally, he'd use both pedals at once. Kurt's settings on the SansAmp's DIP switches were, from left to right, three up, three down, two up, and all of the knobs were turned all of the way up, except for the high control, which was at about 12 o'clock." Vincent does not remember where SansAmp's three-position switch was set, but he thinks it was on the Normal (center) setting.

Vincent says that Cobain would take care of the settings on all of his pedals, sometimes changing them between songs. "He knew all the sweet spots really well," says Vincent. To help get the sounds he wanted more quickly, Cobain marked the different settings on the Echo Flanger and Poly Chorus pedals with nail polish.

Before the band went on tour, Fender sent Cobain one Fiesta Red and three Sonic Blue Mustangs and a variety of Mexican Stratocasters fitted with humbuckers. Bailey installed Gotoh Tune-O-Matic bridges and Seymour Duncan JB humbuckers on the Mustangs, cut the nuts for heavier strings, shimmed the necks, flipped the tailpieces so the strings could be inserted without going under the tailpiece, and blocked the tailpieces so the tremolo bar wouldn't work.

"One of the blue Mustangs never came out of the box and was unmodified because we were waiting until the other ones were broken," says Vincent. "The blue Competition Mustang from *Nevermind* was in storage because Kurt really liked that guitar." However, Cobain had dusted off a few of his Univox Hi-Flyers, and these showed up on stage occasionally.

The Mexican Strats were mainly there for sacrifice to the distortion god at the end of the set. "We had a predetermined black Mexican Strat that we would give to Kurt to smash," says Vincent. "Sometimes he'd want one of the Mustangs, but we wouldn't give him one. Then he'd go, 'Yeah, all right. I don't want to break that guitar because it feels really good.' "

Photos taken at various shows give the impression that Cobain had an endless supply of Mustangs and Stratocasters, but Vincent says this is misleading. Kurt's techs were constantly recycling parts from the guitars that he destroyed, and they often pieced instruments together. "Some of these Nirvana gear web sites list a million guitars," says Vincent. "According to Earnie, most of those guitars are the same, only the pickguard, pickups or neck might have been changed."

After completing *In Utero*, Cobain became more interested in acoustic instruments, and he looked for a replacement for his Stella. Before the tour, Cobain bought an early Sixties right-hand Epiphone Texan, and Bailey replaced the guitar's adjustable bridge with a left-hand bridge and a standard saddle. In the fall of '93, he bought a Martin D-18E electric-acoustic flat-top from Voltage Guitar in Los Angeles. An extremely rare late-Fifties model (only 302 were produced), the D-18E is essentially a D-18 with two DeArmond pickups installed at the Martin factory. "Unfortunately, the instrument's pickups were designed with nickel strings in mind, so hearing it with bronze-wound strings was pretty disappointing," Bailey said in the March '95 *GW*. "Our solution was to attach yet another pickup—a Bartolini model 3AV—to the top." This guitar became his main acoustic guitar for the *In Utero* tour and for Nirvana's appearance on MTV's *Unplugged*.

Taped on November 18, 1993, and aired about a month later, Nirvana's *Unplugged* performance proved to be the ultimate coda to Cobain's musical career. Cobain insisted on bringing the Martin to the taping, even though Bailey thought the Epiphone sounded much better. The D-18E was connected to a Small Clone and DS-2 (in a photo on the CD insert, the DS-2 can be seen slightly above the DGC logo) and run into a Twin Reverb, which was used only as a monitor. The Echo Flanger and Poly Chorus were also brought to the rehearsal, but they were not used on the taping because they created too much 60-cycle hum.

In early '94, Fender sent Cobain a sunburst Telecaster Custom. Bailey installed a Duncan JB in the bridge position and a Gibson PAF in the neck position. According to Bailey, this was Cobain's new favorite guitar. He used the guitar for a March, 1994, recording session in his basement with Pat Smear and Hole's Eric Erlandson. This may be the last guitar that Cobain played before he took his own life.

PEARL JAM

Guitar World, September 1992

Alive and Kicking

Pearl Jam has become a media phenomenon, but guitarists Stone Gossard and Mike McCready are playin' it real cool.

By Jeff Gilbert

IN THE BEGINNING, before they began selling truckloads of records in countries they'd never even heard of, Pearl Jam was simply about songs. Songs that were heavily passionate, rich with steady swirls of unforced melody, and tempered by strong, elusive riffs and a purposeful edge. Guitarists Stone Gossard and Mike McCready's spontaneous blend of enigmatic chords and understated lead breaks transcended rock clichés to evoke powerful, genuine emotions. The simple one-note spiral of "Alive" and the hypno-riffing of "Even Flow" clearly demonstrated that this was no ordinary rock group.

When the worldwide rock community embraced the band as leaders of the new grunge revolution, it soon became obvious that Pearl Jam was riding the crest of a tidal wave of valid hype to—could it be?—superstardom. There they were, appearing on *Saturday Night Live* and MTV (with regularity), surfing hitherto alien waters. A Platinum band, hanging *Ten*.

Since last year's album release, the band has toured ceaselessly, journeying around the world. In a decidedly less-than-posh Paris hotel room, Gossard answers the knock of a maid. No black silk stockings. No frilly apron. If the guitarist is disappointed, however, he doesn't show it. Outside, in the cold and damp street beneath his window, a group of kids hope for a chance to get an autograph or photo. Pearl Jam, soaring in the U.S., is also riding high in France—indeed, they are hot all over Europe.

The demands spawned by success have made it nearly impossible for the members of Pearl Jam to enjoy the fruits of that success. "It's almost turned into the job you never wanted in the first place," moans Gossard with a snicker. When *Guitar World* came calling, the band hadn't had a real day off in weeks. It ain't easy, big success. Especially when you have to work this hard.

GUITAR WORLD: Does *Ten*, the title of your album, refer to the months you've spent touring to support it?

STONE GOSSARD: [*laughs*] Man, I'm so burnt out. All I want to do is go home. I'm ready for a long rest.

MIKE McCREADY: We're so tired of talking about ourselves. There's only so much you can say about your band and your guitar.

GW: I take it you're not too caught up in the technical aspects of guitar playing.

McCREADY: I have the worst time doing that. [*laughs*] Guitar magazines ask me technical questions, but I don't know, I just do it! It's more of a feeling thing for me. I totally hate that stuff, it's like math. And I hate math!

GW: Okay, let's talk about something you enjoy doing. Pearl Jam's performance on *MTV Unplugged* must have struck you as a great opportunity to showcase another side of the group.

McCREADY: It came out all right, but it could have been a nightmare because we ordered some specific equipment and they gave us pretty shitty stuff. I wanted to get a Martin, some nice guitars. But when you rent equipment, you don't know what you're getting. Jeff [*Ament, Pearl Jam's bassist*] ordered some specific basses and they didn't appear. The acoustic guitar I played had really high action, so it was totally impossible to do leads. But I thought it came out pretty well anyhow.

GW: Was it equally uncomfortable for you, Stone?

GOSSARD: No. It was a lot scarier going in than it actually turned out to be. We showed up, and instead of the Gibson Chet Atkins steel-string guitar I had ordered, they had a classical one there. It was getting late—like eleven o'clock at night—and where can you rent stuff at that hour? Luckily, we knew some people who were able to score us a couple more guitars, and it turned out fine. I ended up getting the Chet Atkins steel-string—which played great—and a Takamine that felt pretty good. In those kinds of situations, you just have to play with the hand you're dealt. [*laughs*]

McCREADY: It was weird, because we've only done five or six brief acoustic shows, and it forces you to play differently; you can't rely on feedback. [*laughs*] It forces you to use dynamics, and to look at each song in a different way. Some songs turned out good acoustically, and some just didn't quite happen. I didn't think "Even Flow" was any good.

GOSSARD: An acoustic show is really sort of a naked, exposed way of playing your songs, because you can't hide behind distortion. Doing it in front of millions of people is even more intimidating. We actually went out there and had a fun, energized show. It's a cool way to hear the band, because the drums and the vocals are featured a lot more; Dave [Abbruzzese], our drummer, is a great player and Eddie [Vedder] can really shine when he's given room to move around vocally. It gave people a different perception of the band.

GW: How would you rate your performance on *Saturday Night Live*?

McCREADY: I felt good about it. I thought "Porch" was good, and "Alive" was okay. But, honestly, I was nervous as shit. I'm just glad we got through it in one piece.

GW: Did it complicate matters that sex goddess Sharon Stone [*Basic Instinct*] was the guest host?

McCREADY: [*laughs*] Stone's guitar tech, Skully, got her blouse after a sketch where she had to take off her clothes. We took turns smelling it.

GW: Ah, the perks of fame. Did you feel at all mechanical during the performance?

McCREADY: I felt really nervous during the soundcheck before the show, but when we did it, it just felt like playing live. You can't allow yourself to think, "Oh my God...I'm playing in front of 25 million people!" If you do, you'll just freak out. There was definitely a lot of tension—it was a nerve-wracking experience—but just being there was amazing. Me and a buddy went up in one of the rooms and got loaded in honor of John Belushi.

GOSSARD: They bring in a studio audience for a complete dress rehearsal before doing the actual show, and I think the first time we played, we were totally spot-on. But when we did it live, we just sort of jumped out there. I guess it turned out all right—everyone said it was cool—but it wasn't a memorable performance on a guitar level. [*laughs*]

GW: Does your awareness that you've sold over a million records change the way you perform?

GOSSARD: Well, I've always felt pressure to play well live and to be in a great band, so it hasn't really changed things that much. The only thing that affects me is when they charge a lot of money for the show. We've made it a point to try and keep our ticket costs down, but you really want to put on a good show for someone who's paid 20 bucks for a ticket. That's pretty expensive. So I feel a responsibility in that sense.

GW: Now that you've had to live with *Ten* for over a year, does the material still hold up for you?

McCREADY: I think we're much better now, live, than we are on the record. The record is fine for what it is—we were a band for only three and a half months when we recorded it—but I don't think it's the best we can do. We've been working on new songs and have developed a lot of material, so I'm way more excited about doing the next album. I'm really amazed that *Ten* is doing so well.

GW: Have you been prepping with demos or do you just store up jams and ideas?

McCREADY: It's not so much demos as it is working out stuff at soundchecks. We've added two new songs to our set—"Footsteps" and "Drop a Leash." We use the spontaneity to work out kinks.

GOSSARD: We have lots of new songs. You wait and see, you'll be giving our next record high praise! [*laughs*] It's really going to be special. Having Dave in the band has given us a whole new groove and a lot of new types of jams—a lot of different tunings, weirder stuff.

GW: Tell me about "Breath" and "State of Love and Trust," the two songs you have on the *Singles* movie soundtrack.

GOSSARD: They were recorded last February in Seattle, and are just a couple of songs that we thought would be good for the soundtrack. Not much of a story, is it? [*laughs*] They're older songs. "Breath" is on the first demo we did as a band. I used a Les Paul and Marshall on that track. We didn't really have time to mess around and bring in my Vox AC30 and my Steinberger! [*laughs*] We had a day and a half to do it, so I just played through my normal set-up.

GW: In *Singles*, Pearl Jam appear as Matt Dillon's band, Citizen Dick. I haven't seen the movie yet; do you get to play?

GOSSARD: No, we didn't play in the movie at all. Matt Dillon never sings in the movie, either. All the scenes with Matt and Citizen Dick have them sitting around a coffee table, talking or just finishing practice. The only bands that got to play were Soundgarden and Alice in Chains, who appear in the background in bar scenes.

GW: Tell me the story behind "Dirty Frank," the funky B-side of the "Even Flow" single.

McCREADY: "Dirty Frank" was written while we were touring with the Red Hot Chili Peppers. It's about our bus driver, Frank—we were convinced he was a serial killer. We would find piles of empty beer cans under his seat after a whole night's drive. It was like, "Oh man, I'm glad we're still alive!"

GOSSARD: "Dirty Frank" is a Pearl *jam*. The lyrics on that song are amazing, some of the best Eddie's ever written.

GW: The song has a real funk feel to it, no doubt reflecting the influence of touring with the Chili Peppers.

GOSSARD: It had a lot to do with that. You can't help but be influenced by the Chili Peppers when you watch them night after night. Rather than emulating them, we just wanted to catch their groove and feel it the way they feel it. There's a little Chili Peppers tribute in the song, in the line: "They cook 'em just to see the look on their face." A little hats-off tribute. [*laughs*] It's cool to have lighter moments like that. Sometimes it's great to be dark and foreboding, but this band definitely has a sense of humor, too. It's important that it comes out at least every once in a while, to keep things in perspective. I don't think Pearl Jam are doomsday predictors or sad guys; I think we're a band that enjoys life.

GW: With Pearl Jam doing so well, I don't think it surprised too many people to see the re-release of the Temple of the Dog album you did with Chris Cornell and Matt Cameron of Soundgarden last year.

GOSSARD: I think it was really predictable. [*laughs*] It may seem crass, but I'm happy about it, because I think it's an amazing record. I'm really proud of having played and worked on it with Chris and Matt. It's about getting together and having a good time, playing music with some friends you don't normally get a chance to play with.

GW: Are there plans to promote it this time around?

GOSSARD: I don't think anyone's up for touring to support it right now. [*laughs*] I think we've all had our load of touring at this point.

GW: As it is, you'll have two more months of touring with Lollapalooza. What are your impressions of the other bands on the Lollapalooza bill?

McCREADY: I don't really know Ministry that well, but I'm looking forward to checking out Ice Cube, who blows me away. Man, his album is incredible. It's such honest music, with awesome grooves— those old Parliament samples are incredible. That, and Soundgarden, of course. It's always awesome to see them play night after night. The Peppers are an amazing band, and they were really cool to us when we toured together; they went out of their way to take care of us. Eddie incited riots a couple of times, and we were going to be forced to pay for the damage, but the Peppers took care of it. We really love playing with them.

GOSSARD: I think the Lollapalooza lineup is great. Ice Cube is probably the most exciting for me, too, just because I'm such a huge fan. Right now, he makes the greatest rap records around. I'm really interested in seeing how his show comes across live. Other than that, any time you have the Chili Peppers and Soundgarden together, it's going to be cool. Ministry could be interesting; I've never seen them live, but I've heard great things about them. I hear their singer [Al Jourgensen] is a totally "out there" dude. I have no idea whatsoever what Lush and The Jesus and Mary Chain are like. My impression is that they're a little more low-key than the rest of us.

JERRY CANTRELL of ALICE IN CHAINS

Guitar World, January 1992

Rain Man

Alice in Chains' Jerry Cantrell cleans up his act and hits pay *Dirt*.

by Jeff Gilbert

HE SKY IS always crying in Seattle. Like leaden harbingers of gloom, assembly lines of dirty-gray clouds settle in to relieve themselves over the city. Local inhabitants walk in the rain, grimly muttering, "It's another piss-pour day."

The music of Seattle—foreboding, dirty, and loud—is a grim metaphor for the weather. And with his monotone, heavy-lidded eyes and unsmiling demeanor, Alice in Chains guitarist Jerry Cantrell seems in his own way to be a living embodiment of Seattle's somber sky. But behind his desolate exterior, Cantrell masks a wry sense of humor, and even a brooding sort of charm. Certainly anyone who listens to an Alice in Chains album knows that far more is going on inside the guitarist's head than is written on his face.

After exorcising his Kiss and AC/DC demons on *Facelift*, Alice in Chains' 1990 red-hot debut, Cantrell bared the moody and enigmatic essence of his guitarist's soul on the acoustic EP, *Sap*. While his playing was hardly revolutionary in a technical sense, Cantrell's guitar work on *Sap* represented a personal breakthrough melodically, harmonically and conceptually.

Cantrell takes his achievement on *Sap* to an even higher level on *Dirt*, Alice in Chains' second full-length release. Darker and heavier than *Facelift*, and as boldly innovative as *Sap, Dirt* is loaded with bold arrangements, sensory-numbing tones and riffs, and groundbreaking vocal harmonies. The bulldozing chord-ripping of "Them Bones"; the deft, sensitive acoustic strumming of "Down in a Hole"; and the psychedelic roller-coaster ride of "Sickman" collectively stand as a blazing milestone for Cantrell as a guitarist, songwriter and vocalist.

"*Dirt* is the best album I could have made with the best musicians I know," says Cantrell, a rare smile lighting his benighted features.

The coming year should see clear skies and smooth sailing for Alice in Chains, what with the tremendous success of *Dirt* (it shipped Gold) and a prominent cameo appearance by the band in the hit movie *Singles*. Furthermore, the film's popular soundtrack features "Would?" the band's biggest AOR hit to date. "We're already getting offers to do another movie," chuckles Cantrell. "But we've got some touring to do first."

That's the thing with Seattle bands—when it rains, it pours.

GUITAR WORLD: With a new album, two hit songs, "Would?" and "Them Bones," and the *Singles* movie out at the same time, you certainly are in an enviable position. Talk about hitting the ground running...

JERRY CANTRELL: Exactly. It couldn't be any better for us; we're in a real good spot right now. A lot of it was planned, but most of it was luck—it all came together at the right time. And *Singles* is a great movie, real nice and pleasant. I'm totally in love with Bridget Fonda.

GW: Same here. So let's begin with your new album, *Dirt*.

CANTRELL: It turned out so damn good...

GW: Was it any more difficult in the studio for you this time around, especially in terms of any extra pressure your success with *Facelift* may have created?

CANTRELL: No. It was a lot easier because we really didn't think about how we wanted the songs to go down. We went in with the basic idea, but stayed more true to the demo tapes than we did the first time. This album was a lot more free-form, like, "Let's just throw out some ideas, and just put something down." We kept doing it. All of these ideas kept piling up, and by the time it was done, it was just so fucking massive it blew me away. I was really proud to be in this band and playing with Layne [*Staley, singer*], Sean [*Kinney, drummer*] and Mike [*Starr, bassist*]. They rock.

GW: *Dirt* is heavier than *Facelift* and quite a bit darker. Some of the song titles—well, they might lead people to draw certain conclusions about the band. If nothing else, the album seems very personal.

CANTRELL: You're right. It is very personal, especially the songs on the second half—"Junkhead," "God Smack" and "Sickman." They were written as a trilogy-type thing, actually a story, all the way from "Junkhead" to "Angry Chair." "Junkhead" is a pretty blatant song—it sounds like we're flying the flag for drug use. But the whole point is that a lot of people believe that it's great to go out and get fucked up; they reflect the attitude of somebody who's partying and using. "God Smack" starts getting into the realization of what the fuck is really up, and the story moves all the way down into "Angry Chair" and "Hate to Feel," where you realize that this is not the right way to live. Taken as a whole, it's a really positive thing, but a lot of people will probably take it out of context.

GW: It sounds like you're purging a lot of internal poisons with these songs.

CANTRELL: That's the whole thing. Without getting too heavy into this whole drug thing, our music has always been an outlet for feelings that we can't or won't express verbally. People hold things in, and we do, too; we're no different than anybody else. Holding those bad feelings in will just eat you away. We're lucky to have an outlet that we can put this stuff into, and I think that's why a lot of people can relate to our music—it really means something to us. It's an exorcising of demons. I think the majority of our fans understand that and, by listening to us, purge some stuff themselves. Something doesn't have to be physical to be addictive.

GW: What would you say is most distinctive about Alice in Chains? Layne's vocals are unique, as is your approach to the guitar and sound.

CANTRELL: I think both of those things are distinctive—and they go hand in hand. Our music has grown more because we've grown more. The guitar riffs on "Hate to Feel" and "Angry Chair" are some of the sickest riffs on the album, and those are Layne's songs—he wrote those on guitar and he plays them live.

GW: Layne plays guitar?

CANTRELL: Totally. We're all growing as players, including Layne. And he's helped me grow as a singer. Powerful back-up vocals have been something that we've really lacked live, and that's something I'm working on. As for those things we're known for—our trademarks—the reason they're so much more immense this time is that we've really just naturally evolved.

GW: You did a fair amount of the lead vocals on *Sap*. On *Dirt*, you take that two steps further.

CANTRELL: Yeah, I did, and it's really cool. And it happened because of some elbowing from Layne. I write some of the lyrics, and singing them can be difficult for Layne. At the same time, writing for someone else from his point of view—even if that someone is like your brother, as Layne is—will sometimes mean that you fall short in interpretation. Fortunately, I've been able to write stuff that we can all relate to. But I've also written some things where Layne said, "Well, why don't you sing it, man?"

GW: How did [*producer*] Dave Jerden help flesh out both your vocals and Layne's?

CANTRELL: I think the vocals are a lot more pure and raw on this album, totally in your face, which is something Dave was going for. But beyond Dave's great work, Layne just sang like a mother. You can't deny a great singer, and Layne's one of the best I've ever heard. The first time I heard him sing, I hunted his ass down and made him join my band. [*laughs*] He blows me away every time. He's skinny as a rail, yet he sounds like a 350-pound bearded slob, a big ol' fat guy. [*laughs*] I trip on that all the time.

GW: *Sap*, which showed a deep, soulful, acoustic side of the band, confused many of the people who knew you from stuff like "Man in the Box" and "It Ain't Like That."

CANTRELL: Well, a lot of people didn't even know we put it out until way after, which was intentional. We didn't want any ads or promotion—we just put it in the stores to see if anyone would buy it. That way, people would know about it via word of mouth, and there wouldn't be a bunch of people standing around scratching their heads, going, "Man, they really wimped out!" [*laughs*]

It was Sean's idea to put it together, and it worked out really cool. I think the majority of people understood what it was about—demonstrating that we're not just some metal band. While that is what we are at times, we're also a lot more than that: We like to play a lot of different kinds of music.

GW: *Sap* also features "Right Turn," an amazing song with some major league guest vocalists. How did the session with Chris Cornell [*Soundgarden*], Mark Arm [*Mudhoney*] and Ann Wilson [*Heart*] come about?

CANTRELL: That's one of my favorites. It wasn't even something that anybody thought about, really. We'd finished four of the songs on *Sap*, and were just sitting there one night, when I said, "What do you think about bringing Ann in to sing on a couple of tunes, and maybe Chris, and anybody else we can find?" We're really big fans of both Heart and Soundgarden.

I didn't think Chris would show up because he had some things going at the time. I didn't know Mark very well, but I got his number from Layne and called him up, and called Ann, and they all showed up within an hour of my phoning them. I was really surprised. They all whacked out their shit in an hour or two, and it was done. Mark's voice on "Right Turn" gives me the chills—it's like the voice of death. [*laughs*] I gave Chris the words, and Layne and Mark added their own thing to it. It turned out to be one of the most unbelievable songs we've ever done, I think. Very spontaneous.

GW: *Sap* serves as a bridge between *Facelift* and *Dirt*. The new album has strong elements of both records.

CANTRELL: You're exactly right. I'm at a loss for adjectives to describe *Dirt*. Basically, by reaching into the depths, we went lower, musically, than we've ever been. At the same time we also found some really cool and good things about ourselves. At first, going through the whole experience of having a successful first album was kind of hard to accept. It's like, "I'm not worthy!" [*laughs*] It's easy to beat yourself up about it because it's so fake. You're just this thing on a tape and a face on a piece of paper. People forget you're a person, and you forget you're a person. But there came a realization that, yes, I am worth this. I do deserve this. I've worked hard and I'm good.

GW: Daily affirmation with Jerry Cantrell.

CANTRELL: [*laughs*] Absolutely!

GW: *Dirt* is also a very mature record.

CANTRELL: Don't make us sound like we're toothless and gray! [*laughs*]

GW: By mature I mean that where you formerly were bludgeoning riffsters, now you're song craftsmen. Instead of building around a really cool riff, you place more emphasis on songs and song structure.

CANTRELL: You are right. [*laughs*]

GW: The songs "God Smack" and "Sickman," in particular, exemplify all this growing and experimentation, the advanced songwriting skills, the different types of guitar tones...

CANTRELL: There's a lot of different stuff in both those tunes. For the guitar tones, I used my Bogners, a Mesa/Boogie Dual Rectifier, and a Rockman; last time I used the Marshalls modified by Bogner, which is what I use live. And instead of EQing the guitar, I put down guitar tracks of different EQ sounds. I put the low stuff with the Dual Rectifier, the big whomping shit, and the real biting stuff that is my sound in the middle, and then a real shitty, high Rockman on top of it. I did this on each side, so that even though there's three tracks on each side, they're not necessarily used every time. But whatever sound you want, instead of having to twist the knob, it's already there. That was due to Dave Jerden; he's a really smart guy.

GW: Jerden, like Terry Date [*Soundgarden, Pantera*], understands the strengths of the band he's working with and allows them to fulfill their potential without screwing with their sound.

CANTRELL: Exactly on the mark. Terry and Dave are on the exact same, very high, level. Thom Panunzio, the guy who did the War

Babies album, is like that, too.

GW: *Dirt* really showcases your talents, especially the acoustic song, "Down in a Hole," which hit me the way some of the tracks on *Sap* did.

CANTRELL: That thing gives me the chills, but I didn't think it would even make the record. I wrote it about a girl I went out with for some time and really dug a lot. It was a pretty song, and when I brought it in I thought there was no way the guys were gonna let me put it on the album. [*laughs*] When we recorded it, I used a 12-string guitar, and it was like, "Damn, that's the prettiest, most beautiful song I ever heard!" I can't believe the band likes it. [*laughs*] For something to get on the record, the whole band's really got to be jazzed on it. Fortunately, they were.

I used Taylor six- and 12-strings and a classical guitar on there. I just bought a Taylor, and it's a great, very warm-sounding guitar.

GW: What other new toys did you use?

CANTRELL: Dave's really into collecting old effects, like the stuff Jimi Hendrix used. We used a lot of these old Vox pedals, flanging chorus pedals. On "Down in a Hole," we ran an acoustic through these ancient flangers and a chorus and it sounded great.

GW: Your use of the wah is more understated this time around.

CANTRELL: I used it quite a bit, but maybe not as blatantly as I did on *Facelift*. It's just blending in a little more and supporting everything instead of sticking out. I love CryBaby wah—it's my main, number-one effect. It makes the guitar talk, so it was great sticking it out on *Facelift*. But now I'm going for a different sound and tone. I also used some different CryBabys. When we were touring with Van Halen, Dunlop gave me a pedal that was designed after a Hendrix and Jeff Beck wah sound, kinda muddy and rich-sounding, not as transistory...

GW: Like...dirt?

CANTRELL: [*laughs*] Precisely! They sound like mud. I'm really proud of the sounds on this record, and not in a cock-walkin' way. It blows me away.

GW: Speaking of being blown away, "Sickman" has all these unbelievably wild vocal and guitar parts.

CANTRELL: Layne said, "I want to write some really insane lyrics, so I need the most insane, wild, out-there music you've ever done." So I put together all these riffs I had. It was so disjointed, but I showed them to Mike and Sean—and they just wigged out and took it way further than I thought it would go. Then we gave it to Layne, and that's how it turned out. Layne specifically requested a certain mood and we were able to come up with it. There's this crunchin' metal stuff, a psycho-circus polka, a speed-metally, dreamy, drugged-out weird sound after that, and then a real weird chorus. It's a trip. It's real powerful live.

GW: What are the equipment changes this time out?

CANTRELL: I got rid of my VHT power amps because they were a little too dark—and muddy-sounding. I mean, they sound great, but the way I have it set with the preamps, I needed a solid-state thing. So I switched to MosValves. It gave me a little more crispness and crunch. The only thing I used for effects last time was my P.C. Electronics thing, and I shit-canned that because it was too complicated to figure out. [*laughs*] I got these two Rocktron multi-effects units, and a Hush system to quiet it out a little. A pretty simple system.

GW: How about guitars? I know you're using the Eddie Van Halen Ernie Ball guitar now.

CANTRELL: I love that thing, I play it all the time. Eddie gave me that guitar and a bunch of other stuff. He's a generous guy. It was like, "What do you want, a couple of stacks?" I said, "No man, just a head would be great; I'll buy it off you." And he goes, "Fuck that, man! I'll just give it to you." When I didn't have anything, nobody would give me shit. And now that I have everything, everybody wants to give me stuff. [*laughs*] Eddie's very cool; he loaded me up with a couple stacks of his Peavey 5150 stuff and gave me a guitar and a practice amp. He gave me more gear than I had. [*laughs*] He's a real sweetheart. He hung out in our room more than he hung with his own band.

GW: Yeah, well, who would want to hang out with Sammy Hagar?

CANTRELL: [*laughs*] Oh, hey, he's great, too. But Eddie had some fun hanging out with us. It's an amazing thing to deal with, but it's kind of cool.

GW: Does it boggle your brain to have toured with Van Halen, and to find an enthusiastic fan in Eddie?

CANTRELL: Yeah. It goes back to what we were talking about before: You gotta have a certain amount of confidence to do this type of work. And when you start meeting people you've really looked up to for years, and you end up being friends with them out of mutual respect for each other's music, it's pretty hard to deal with. Again, you have to realize you're worth that. You've created something that's touched somebody else. It's really gratifying.

EDDIE VEDDER of PEARL JAM

The Mouths That Scored

It takes a big heart and a healthy set of lungs to be the voice of a generation. Pearl Jam's Eddie Vedder and Soundgarden's Chris Cornell explain.

By Jeff Gilbert

WHAT A LONG, strained trip it's been. During the course of this musically tedious and tumultuous year, we've watched—with guarded patience—two of Seattle's favorite homeboys, Soundgarden and Pearl Jam, inch their way toward global domination, like big, hairy slugs hot on the trail of rotting fruit. In the process, they've sold more records than a dead Elvis, swung their hair around on *Saturday Night Live*, and hung out with Guns N' Roses frontman Axl Rose. Seems you can't pick up a magazine anymore that doesn't have a fold-out shot of Chris Cornell's buff torso or Eddie Vedder hanging from a lighting rig.

This year, both Pearl Jam and Soundgarden will play feature roles in Lollapalooza II, a *wunderfest* of politically correct music and politically correct politics—a Woodstock Lite for the Nineties (same great bands, 1/3 less guitar solos). As it did last year, the headline-making event will feature all sorts of monstrously great bands and propaganda-spewing booths, dotting concert sites like ripe field mushrooms.

If the patently white funk of the Red Hot Chili Peppers doesn't move you to dance, or the mechanized syncopations of Ministry fail to realign your sense of reality, you'll still be able to do things like buy "made in Korea" T-shirts printed with the *cause du jour*, publicly smoke pot without fear, resurrect the peace sign (still two fingers) and visit consciousness-raising booths like Rock the Vote (to register), Rock for Choice (to support the right to choose) and the popular Rock the Environment (to learn to drink beer from an aluminum container outdoors without feeling guilty). Then there's the Rock the Grunge booth, where you can sponsor a poor, outta state musician and send him (or her) to Seattle to score a record deal. Lollapalooza has something for everyone—especially for fans of Soundgarden and Pearl Jam.

Pearl Jam and Soundgarden are international phenomena now; reaching them meant calling halfway around the world. Chris Cornell had a cold and was cooped up writing new songs in his room at the Düsseldorf Ramada Inn, a stop on Soundgarden's European tour in support of Guns N' Roses. Eddie Vedder, meanwhile, had just come off a stage in Hamburg, where Pearl Jam headlined a sold-out 50,000-seat festival. After doing a lengthy interview with a surfer magazine, he was still wide awake enough to chat.

EDDIE VEDDER

GUITAR WORLD: Has success made you a working man against your will?

EDDIE VEDDER: Are you kidding? It's work, but no work gets rewards like this. Communicating with people—I guess that's always been a thing of mine, to communicate to the numbers of people and have them sing along. I was listening last night to the tape of our show and there were parts when the audience was singing louder than I was.

GW: Do you find it surprising that people react as they do to your songs?

VEDDER: I'm very surprised. I've never really written for people, just for myself. And the fact that anybody, anywhere, has responded to this at all is very surprising. In a very unexpected way, it's gratifying. I don't mean to sound all soapy and stuff, but coming from a pretty troubled past, it makes something so positive like this more overwhelming.

GW: By "troubled past," do you mean family?

VEDDER: I thought it would be a good thing to say in interviews. [*laughs*] It makes it more intriguing. Jesus Christ, if it weren't for music, I wouldn't have survived any of it. Maybe that's why the stakes are so high with me—music's everything.

GW: At some early Pearl Jam performances that I saw, you seemed to be harmonious and content—not taken over by it all. Yet at recent concerts, it seems like you have developed an inner anger, a harder edge.

VEDDER: Having seen more of what's around me and what's going on in this country and the world, I can't really be happy about it. I can't really kick back and sing about how life is good and everything is good, while all I see is tragedy around me, to the point where I could easily let it catch me in a downward spiral and suck me under. It's all this shit that's going on, and I'm totally involved with it. I'm meeting these people first-hand, and I'm reading these letters from people who somehow relate to our songs in some tragic manner.

GW: Tragic?

VEDDER: There was a girl in a wheelchair who showed up at soundcheck at one of our shows. I was riding my skateboard around the empty floor while the opening band was doing their soundcheck, and I rode up to her and said, "Oh, you've got some wheels, too." We started talking and she broke down, saying how she'd been in a really bad accident and that the song "Alive" gave her strength to carry on. And it's just really intense; you go out and sing it harder than ever. It means so much more than it did when it was just a song. I walk up onstage with a whole lot of baggage, and you gotta sing it as hard as you can just to get it out. I'm not just singing for myself anymore.

GW: Seems like a heavy burden to lug around.

VEDDER: In a way it seems like that. But it makes the art so much more powerful, now that I think about it. At times it gets way too heavy and you think, "What the fuck am I doing? I'm just a little guy; I can't carry all this," or "I can't live up to these expectations." But that's just me; I've always been that way. It's just that the scale of everything has changed, and that's really something we never expected.

GW: You don't sound like you're enjoying the situation.

VEDDER: I can't speak for the rest of the band, but I'm not really happy about it. They know I'm not comfortable with the success of this band. I'd like to make three or four records without anybody knowing who we are, so that the records would be honest. Now there's going to be a hype-thing happening. People are gonna be looking to wrestle with the second record because the whole thing has been blown out of proportion. I'm not gonna give a fuck, I'm gonna write as I always have.

GW: At the end of your performance on *Saturday Night Live*, you turned your back to the camera and pulled your jacket down to reveal a message printed on your shirt. The camera pulled out of range, so no one saw what it was you wanted everyone to see.

VEDDER: The shirt read: "No Bush '92," and the front was just a coat hanger. The cameraman was a Republican and he backed off a little bit and pulled out of range. [*laughs*]

GW: The coat hanger is a symbol for pro-choice.

VEDDER: That is the only cause that I will go public with. We played with Fugazi in Los Angeles at a pro-choice benefit called Rock for Choice where we signed up a whole lot of people to vote and got petitions signed for the RU 486 bill supporting the French abortion pill. You get a chance to say something on national TV, and I'm not gonna keep my mouth shut. I try to do it in a subtle enough way.

GW: Like having the words "pro-choice" written in bold letters on your arms at Pearl Jam's *MTV Unplugged* performance?

VEDDER: Okay, I'm trying to be subtle! [*laughs*] But my emotions sometimes get the best of me. That's something I feel really strongly about, the *quality* of life, not quantity. The people who are making this decision are upper middle-class religious types who don't have to live with it. These are not the people who are going to have to live and die by the decision.

GW: What are your thoughts on HB 2554, the Washington State erotic music bill that was recently overthrown?

VEDDER: At this point, there's gonna be little kids standing outside record stores asking adults to buy them the new Dwarves record. [*laughs*] I bought a T-shirt that says, "I Buy Records for Minors." That's where the hard-core censorship comes in. It could really change the future of music and that's why it's got to stop.

GW: What's the story behind the slagging Pearl Jam received from *New Music Express*, one of London's biggest music publications?

VEDDER: *NME* said that Pearl Jam was trying steal money from young alternative kids' pockets. It really kind of bugged me, and I didn't want to say anything and get in a pissing match with anybody. But someone told me about it a half hour before the show, and when I got on stage, halfway through the set, I said, "*NME* says we're trying to steal your money. Don't buy the record, tape it off your friends. In fact, I hope there's bootleggers here who can make tapes and sell them. We want you to make money off this band...we don't give a fuck!" It's fucking music, you know? I think it's bullshit that anyone's gonna go out and try to tell people what they should be listening to.

GW: Maybe Pearl Jam are easy targets because you do sell a lot of records. Maybe it's just part of the "Seattle scene" backlash.

VEDDER: We're into the backlash thing, too! [*laughs*] We're sick of it! I feel silly, anyway, because I'm from San Diego and the whole time I've spent in Seattle has been in a basement of an art gallery with no windows, writing songs. That's how much of Seattle I've seen. We're all really, really sick of the whole "Seattle scene" thing. And I don't think it's something anybody asked for. It's nothing Soundgarden asked for and it's certainly not something that we asked for. It's rare and cool and something to be proud of. Too bad they put it on *Entertainment Tonight* and embarrassed us all. [*laughs*]

GW: It must be great, then, to be a part of Lollapalooza II, a celebration of musical diversity and information. Do you think the concert will have the same kind of social relevance that it did last year?

VEDDER: I hope so. Actually, I'm not as excited about playing as I am about hanging out with all the other artists and meeting non-musicians and going around to all the booths and things like that. I have a backpack, the same backpack I take to Yosemite, and a skateboard, and I'm just gonna cruise around and hang out and be like a bohemian. Playing will be just, like, one thing you do for 45 minutes.

GW: What else bothers you?

VEDDER: I wish we weren't on MTV, man. It's just weird how there are things you can't control. All of a sudden it gets out of hand, and you're standing there going, "Fuck." So what do you do? You play emotionally correct because you can, then you turn it into something else. You gotta be honest. And I just feel silly talking about our band all the time. There are so many great bands—you hate talking about yourself and want to talk about the new Buffalo Tom or Henry Rollins records.

GW: The *Singles* movie, in which Pearl Jam is featured both on screen and on the soundtrack, is going to make it tough for you to talk about anything else for awhile.

VEDDER: People really get mad at me for saying this, but Mudhoney has an amazing song on the soundtrack that is a disclaimer for the whole thing. It's called "Overblown." God, the last verse is just so perfect: [*sings*] "Everybody loves us/we're getting pretty old/can't hold a regular job/long live rock and roll!" Classic! [*laughs*]

GW: I can't help but think it's more than just a coincidence how *Singles*, which features just about every prominent band in Seattle, came out at the same time the Seattle music-scene thing blew up.

VEDDER: The whole Seattle thing has gotten so ridiculously out of control since we did the movie, which was almost two years ago. If Warner Bros., or whoever, says anything about the Seattle scene on any billboard or ad, I'm gonna go to a state where you can buy a rifle and drive to Los Angeles and blow somebody's head off. [*laughs*] I'll be the martyr.

CHRIS CORNELL

GUITAR WORLD: You've been on the road with Guns N' Roses, on and off, for some time now. Is touring with them as chaotic as it appears?

CHRIS CORNELL: Not really. On average, we play two shows a week with Guns. They don't like to play that much and they lose a lot of money. We could go do our own shows, I suppose, but I really don't want to. [*laughs*] I'd rather do some writing. It's kind of like a vacation, just staying in my room, writing songs. I haven't really done anything else the whole time we've been touring. I don't really like touring around Europe; it's kind of boring. You can drink and then go look at something. [*laughs*] If I stay in my room and write songs, it's like I'm at home. The only way I can tell that I'm not home is if I look out the window.

GW: Has touring stopped being fun for you?

CORNELL: You mean, "Has it *started* being fun?" It hasn't been that hard this time out. It hasn't been as hard as the *Louder Than Love* tour. I think you get used to it. We used to do 17 shows in a row; you can't really do that anymore when you're headlining. As it's ended up, we get a week off at home every six or seven weeks, which is really cool. That's the thing that keeps it from being a complete drag. But you can't get into being at home because you don't remember what to do when you're there. I usually drink a lot when I'm home every day, because I don't drink when I'm on tour. As long as I don't drive, it's not too stupid. I don't try to solve the world's problems when I'm drunk, either. Driving and solving the world's problems when you're drunk—those things don't work. It's like you're waking up at four in the morning, vomiting, trying to remember how it was you discovered the cure for AIDS..."What was that I said?...bleeaarrgghh!!" [*laughs*]

GW: In the issue of *RIP* magazine that had you on the cover, editor Lonn Friend made a statement that said Seattle has more heroin users per capita than any other city in the United States. Where did he come up with that?

CORNELL: Part of it might be because [*singer*] Andy Wood died from a drug overdose, and Lonn was a really big Mother Love Bone fan; that really bummed him out. Then there's all the rumors about the guys in Mudhoney and Nirvana and all that shit. In that interview I was basically saying I don't do drugs, but that doesn't mean I'm this together, well-adjusted, rock star guy, because that's not true; I'm as fucked-up as anybody. I just don't do drugs. It's as simple as that. Maybe Lonn was trying to understand why other people did it. To me, it's a relatively clean scene compared to some.

I think the other point to be made is that I don't believe musicians and rock stars have any kind of responsibility to be role models for anybody. The only responsibility they have is to be true to what they're doing artistically and not use any kind of production or packaging techniques to fool people into buying records, like Milli Vanilli did. To me, those guys are way worse than somebody whose idol is on drugs. I don't think any celebrity is responsible for setting an example to young people. If you're looking for role models, maybe you should be into Michael Jordan, because he seems to be into being one.

GW: Let's talk about the worldwide Pay-Per-View cable broadcast Soundgarden performed with Guns N' Roses in Paris. That was some serious exposure.

CORNELL: No shit! But those people aren't running out to buy our records. If they were, we'd be selling millions of records, and it's obvious we're not. It's just another inch inside the door. I think that's how bands with longevity end up doing it. It's kind of like what the Cure did in the U.S.; U2 did the same thing. For Soundgarden, that's all it is, those kinds of tours and playing in front of an audience that isn't ours.

GW: A&M is planning to re-release the *Temple of the Dog* record and treat it as a new album.

CORNELL: Everyone was paranoid when we first released that album. It was more of a commercial record than our next record was going to be, and we didn't want to cheapen it by releasing it as members of this band and that band. It was before Pearl Jam had anything out, and no one really knew who they were. No one really wanted to stick his neck out and push *Temple*. It was more like, "Let's throw it out there."

GW: It doesn't hurt now that both Soundgarden and Pearl Jam are selling records and doing so well.

CORNELL: Yeah, now it's not as much of a risk. Both bands have gotten all this exposure, so no one's gonna mistake it for something other than what it is. No one's going to say, "That's Chris Cornell's new band." *Temple* is a thing we did together; it should be cool.

GW: Another record coming out soon, the *Singles* soundtrack, featuring Pearl Jam, Soundgarden and your solo track, "Seasons," should do really well, too.

CORNELL: I hope so. The timing seems right.

GW: It was rumored that you wrote "Seasons" and some other songs as a joke using fictional titles Jeff Ament [*Pearl Jam*] created for an album used in the movie.

CORNELL: I just did it as a surprise for Cameron [*Crowe, the film's director*]. I did it partly because I had always wanted to do that—write down 10 titles on a piece of paper and make an album based on those titles. One day when I was on the movie set, I saw the cassette lying there with the titles on it. It was the Cliff Poncier fictitious solo tape, and I thought it would be really fun to whip out some quick four-track shit and make this thing real and give it to Cameron as a surprise. The songs were totally influenced by the titles and my interpretation of the vibe of what solo tapes are like. Solo tapes usually have lame production and a lot of acoustic shit, and softer, more inside views of whoever's writing it.

GW: You could have a career on the coffee-house circuit as a solo act with those songs.

CORNELL: [*laughs*] I'm too shitty of a guitar player to do that.

GW: You also contributed music to the film's score.

CORNELL: Yeah, but I don't know how much of it they used.

GW: *Screaming Life* has now been reissued as part of the Sub Pop Classics series. Does it feel strange to have enough popular history to warrant a reissue?

CORNELL: As long as they pay us for it, it's fine. [*laughs*] I don't know how I feel. I'm not the kind of guy who gloats much on the history of what I've done and what the band has done. That kind of thing scares me. When you start thinking about that, the future kind of gets away from you. To have that kind of history, it's hard to look back and think, "Wow, we really accomplished a lot," because I've never been surprised by our success or anything we've ever done. It all sort of makes sense, and happened the way I figured it would.

There hasn't been any overnight success, really. Everything's been slow and pragmatic. I have no clue as to the magnitude of what our history is, the listening audience, or how we're perceived or how I'm perceived. I'm pretty removed from it.

GW: Which seems strange, given that you're in the eye of the hurricane, so to speak.

CORNELL: It's impossible to have that perspective. I suppose I could go out and listen to the fans, and hear what they think and how they react. Maybe I could get a better idea of what we've done. I know there are a lot of fans we've influenced and a lot of rock stars we've influenced. But it's a thing you can never measure in terms of impact. Even if it is a big impact, you can never count on being recognized for it. I know that some day, after this Seattle-scene thing is just completely dead and buried and the most unhip thing in the world—which will happen—at some point in my forties, there's gonna be a resurgence and they're going to start playing all our old videos again. And it'll look like something from the Fifties. [*laughs*] Then there's gonna be some new band that sounds kind of like we did, like what the Black Crowes are to the Stones and the Faces. That will be cool. Then we'll really know if we had any kind of impact. As far as what the Encyclopedia of Rock and Roll will say about us in the year 2010...are we even going to be mentioned, or are we gonna be listed as one of the forerunners of this big, huge, Seattle scene? Or will they just put Nirvana in? Or will they just blow the whole thing off and it will continue to be Jimi Hendrix and Heart and Queensrÿche? [*laughs*] I want to be successful, and I want to think what we're doing is worthwhile; otherwise you have to start questioning why you bother doing it. But I don't wanna be crammed down anybody's throat. I don't wanna be hated; I would rather be hated because I suck. That's fair. Then I could look back and say, "Yeah, we deserved to be hated."

GW: As far as flattery by your peers goes, it was cool to see a Soundgarden press photo taped to Nigel Tufnel's amplifier when Spinal Tap played Seattle.

CORNELL: I heard about that; fuckin' great! I wish we could have been there—I could have worn some kind of Kiss make-up and come out on stage and done a solo without being plugged in. [*laughs*]

GW: During Ice-T's soundcheck when he played Seattle, he yelled at the guy back at the board to turn it up because "This is Soundgarden's town...we gotta be loud!"

CORNELL: That's so cool. We played a show together one time, and he saw us and thought what we were doing was pretty intense. When I lost my temper at that show and kicked a bunch of amps over when we played "Big Dumb Sex," he told us he thought it was cool and over the top. We discussed doing a tour with Body Count [*Ice-T's metal band*], but he was making a record and it never worked out. That would have been a blast.

PEARL JAM

Guitar World, May 1993

Goldfinger

First, there was Mother Love Bone. Then came Temple of the Dog and the phenomenal Pearl Jam. Guitarist Stone Gossard's latest side project is Brad, and all indications are that he still has the magic touch.

By Jeff Kitts

I N AN AGE where an emphasis on "feel over technique" has practically become a religious obligation in rock and roll, Pearl Jam's Stone Gossard has become a High Priest. The bleached, stubby-haired guitarist is today a hero to an entire younger generation of players—players who aspire to make great music without spending hours in a classroom or a month's salary on expensive gear.

Gossard's rapid rise to his current status as one of rock's most respected guitarists began in the mid Eighties, when his work in the band Green River began earning him notoriety in his native Seattle. After the disbandment of the confused, half punk/half glam outfit, Gossard and River bassist Jeff Ament formed Mother Love Bone, which knew a tragically brief existence owing to the death of its singer, Andrew Wood. Gossard's style in Love Bone—a wildly effective hodgepodge of wah-wah chord strumming, ethereal picking and pre-grungy metal riffs—clearly foreshadows his current, highly-renowned approach.

The gap between Gossard's Mother Love Bone days and his current incarnation as Pearl Jam grunge lord was bridged in 1990 by the

Temple of the Dog project. A one-time, collective effort by Gossard, Ament, local singer Eddie Vedder and Soundgarden members Chris Cornell and Matt Cameron, Temple of the Dog recorded one gorgeous, heartfelt album as a tribute to Wood and then split up. Gossard, Ament and Vedder subsequently formed Pearl Jam, with whom Gossard attained multi-platinum heights.

Despite his enviable success, Stone Gossard is a hardened workaholic. During the past holiday season, while his Pearl Jam cohorts were enjoying a much-needed vacation, Stone was immersing himself in yet another band project, a soulful, rhythm-and-blues outfit called Brad. Designating a two-week block of time in which to work without rules, expectations or guidelines, the members of Brad approached the recording of their self-titled album (Epic) as an old-fashioned, experimental jam session.

"We didn't know if we would all get along or if we would be able to write any songs or accomplish anything at all," says Gossard, "but we gave it a shot anyway."

But Brad, like Temple of the Dog, was a one-time-only affair, and Stone is already focusing his attention on the next Pearl Jam album, which is scheduled for release as early as this summer.

"*Ten* is just about on its way out, and we think releasing the next album in July will be good timing. If we make a good record, I don't see any reason why people won't be ready for another Pearl Jam album. People never complain about having too much good music."

Within barely five years, Stone Gossard has already played a leading role in four of rock's most exciting bands: Mother Love Bone, Temple of the Dog, Pearl Jam, and now, in what is perhaps his most curious project, Brad. Be it a testament to his tasteful playing, some magical power, or pure luck, it is apparent that everything Stone Gossard touches turns to gold—and, sometimes, even Platinum.

GUITAR WORLD: The Temple of the Dog and Brad albums were both written and recorded rather quickly. Do you prefer working under pressure?

STONE GOSSARD: I think there's something to be said for working quickly. I don't think it's the only way to work, or that you will always make a better album if you do it fast, but there definitely is something that comes out of working spontaneously and leaving things raw and unpolished. You shouldn't be ashamed to have mistakes on an album or leave things out of tune—those mistakes can help make an album great.

GW: How did those two one-off projects differ from Pearl Jam's *Ten* album?

GOSSARD: *Ten* was a different kind of album, mainly because Pearl Jam is my primary band. We spent two months recording that album, which, to us, is a very long time. It's easy to plow through things like *Temple* and *Brad* when nothing you do really matters. But Pearl Jam can be a bit more political, and sometimes it requires more time to iron things out.

GW: Is it ever beneficial to labor over something until you get it right?

GOSSARD: Sure. It can be very helpful to beat your head against a wall when you're making a record. There will always be those songs that deserve the extra time to get right, especially if you had a vision of a certain mood or feeling when you first wrote it, and are trying to recreate that feeling in the studio. Part of the process of making a record is to fully immerse yourself in what you're doing and work at it until you feel it's done. You get to the point where you just know when you should either take a break or play a part 50 more times; it all depends on the situation. It's not a very analytical thing...you just go with the feeling at that time.

GW: The Brad album was written and recorded in 17 days. How is it possible to make such a good album so quickly?

GOSSARD: One of the reasons why I feel so good about this album is because it proved that you can make a great album without spending a lot of time on it; it takes away some of the mystique of recording albums. We did it in 17 days and spent about $10,000 on it, and had very little rehearsal time.

GW: How did the material come together?

GOSSARD: We rehearsed for five days, jamming for four or five hours a day, and we just marked down the jams that we liked. After the five days, we went into the studio with seven songs completed and wrote three more in the studio, and that was it. We ended up recording all the songs we set out to record, plus another two that weren't planned. It was just the right amount of time to make the record.

GW: How did that approach differ from the way Pearl Jam compiles material?

GOSSARD: The writing process was a bit more jam-oriented than Pearl Jam—or anything I've ever been involved in, for that matter. Seventy percent of the songs on the Brad album are just pieces of different jams that we assembled. We were able to do it very quickly and efficiently because Shawn [*Smith, singer*] has a very good pop sense and knows how to write and arrange good hooks, and I also know how to arrange things quickly. The whole process was very natural for us.

GW: Do you think you'll apply that approach to the next Pearl Jam album?

GOSSARD: The way we did the Brad album was such a satisfying way to make an album, that I do hope it will carry over into the next Pearl Jam album. The Brad album makes a lot of statements by the individual band members as well as by the entire group, and that's also something I'd like to bring to the next Pearl Jam record.

The Brad album was a good confidence-booster for me. But, since the other guys in Pearl Jam didn't have the same experience, time will tell whether or not the experience I had working with other musicians will be a positive influence on Pearl Jam.

GW: Mother Love Bone, Temple of the Dog, Pearl Jam and Brad have all been blessed with the kind of chemistry that most bands strive for but never fully achieve. How do you account for that?

GOSSARD: I think it has to do with people playing to the strengths of the other band members. You should know what you like about your own playing and how other people play—and have some kind of a vision for how the two styles can blend. I think I do that relatively well. I have a good ear for listening to someone else's style and seeing how my style can mesh with theirs. I also think I've been fortunate to work with people who aren't afraid to take chances and try new things. I think all of those things play a part in making any group of musicians sound like they've been playing together for years.

GW: In the case of Brad, it seems that you basically got a bunch of musicians together and went into the studio to see what you could produce—with no real idea of how it would turn out.

GOSSARD: That's exactly how it was. We knew that we could go in and just fall flat on our faces—but we wanted to try it anyway. That was the theme of the whole project—to expose ourselves to something different and take a chance on something. Now, whenever I face something that seems insurmountable, I'll remember how we made the Brad album and know that I can do just about anything.

GW: When did the idea to get Brad together first come about, and who actually conceived the whole thing?

GOSSARD: I had a little break right before we started the Lollapalooza tour, during which I hung out with Regan [*Hagar, drums*] and Shawn, who were both in this Seattle band called Bliss. I went to see them rehearse one day and we decided to jam. So we wrote a song and it came out really cool and since I had already toyed with the idea of putting another band together and making a record, we decided to do it.

Regan was in Malfunction, which was Andrew Wood's band, and Shawn was also a good friend of Andy's, so we all knew each other from around Seattle. As for Jeremy [*Toback, bass*], we only met him a month before we recorded, and we'd never even heard him play. But that was all part of the experiment.

GW: It seems odd that you would even consider putting another band together, considering how exhausted you were when Lollapalooza started.

GOSSARD: Yeah, but making a record is a completely different process from being on the road. Pearl Jam had already been on the road for a year straight, playing the same songs each night and not really having time to write or generate new ideas. All our tours were really great, but it got to the point where it became more of an obligation—something that I had to do every day. So getting the chance to go back to Seattle for two weeks and jam with a few friends and make a record was my idea of a vacation.

GW: How did the other members of Pearl Jam spend their time off after Lollapalooza?

GOSSARD: Everyone has a lot of interests outside of music, and they didn't all want to handle their time off the way I did. Jeff [*Ament*] is really into art and drawing. He went back to Montana and spent time with his family, and Eddie [*Vedder*] went surfing. Everyone did what they wanted, and I thought it would be exciting to make a record with some different personalities.

GW: How do you feel now?

GOSSARD: Totally rested. I've had some time off; I went to Hawaii for 10 days and did absolutely nothing. I went skiing—and now I'm just totally excited about making the next Pearl Jam album.

GW: Brad's music is much more r&b/soul-oriented than Pearl Jam's. Are you all r&b fans?

GOSSARD: Oh, yeah. Shawn, especially, has a very strong r&b influence—he's totally into Earth, Wind & Fire, Sly Stone, Prince, and Funkadelic. Those kinds of bands played a huge part in making rock music great, and not enough rock bands have singers that are influenced by those bands. I'm not a real aficionado of r&b and soul bands, but I've always appreciated them and known that they've influenced my playing in one way or another. The great fun of rock and roll is combining influences, and that's how the whole thing keeps moving forward.

GW: You've worked with some extraordinary singers like Andrew Wood, Chris Cornell, Eddie Vedder, and now Shawn Smith. Anything you can pinpoint about all of them that attracts you?

GOSSARD: All of them are completely different singers, yet they all have that ability to dig down to that one level below their normal, self-conscious ego and bring something out of themselves that moves you. I know what I like in a singer, and I know what moves me. It just so happens that I've gotten to work with singers who are able to move other people as well. I'm as much of a fan of those guys as anyone.

GW: The original name for the Brad project was Shame. Why did it change?

GOSSARD: Well, it turned out that another band was already called Shame. We tried to buy the rights, but the guy who owned them refused to sell. So we called ourselves Brad—which, coincidentally, was the name of the guy who wouldn't sell. [*laughs*]

GW: As a player, do you find it beneficial to play regularly, or do you need breaks?

GOSSARD: After we finished the Brad album, I didn't even pick up my guitar for a long time. My new thing is playing drums. I bought a drum set, and I think I can be an all right drummer if I put some effort into it. I've been spending a few hours a week just beating on my drums. Even if I never play drums on a record, I just love playing because it's totally therapeutic. Everyone should play drums—it's the great truth-teller. If you're not thinking pure, musical thoughts, you'll play like shit. But if you clear your mind and believe that you can play, you will be able to play. It's a real challenge.

GW: How has that helped you as a guitarist?

GOSSARD: It helps you to see how locked into certain rhythms you are. It's especially useful when you're trying to think of alternative melodies to go over the top of something else. It's interesting to apply the kick-snare-hi-hat beat to your guitar playing. After a while, I learned that the same kinds of things I work out on the drums I could work out on my guitar. It also helps to be able to force something to work rhythmically.

GW: Did you use any studio techniques with Brad that you haven't tried with Pearl Jam?

GOSSARD: We used drum loops on a few songs, and that was a whole new experience for me. I wanted to experiment with them because I love rap, and I love the way drum loops can create a totally different mood within a song. We wrote "20th Century" the way we wrote all the other songs, and we felt that the main aspect of the song was that it was just one repetitive riff; so it seemed like the perfect situation to try a drum loop.

The rest of the recording process was very low-key. We recorded in a really basic, 16-track garage-type studio with all of us in the same room. Half of the album's vocals were recorded live, and a lot of them were done while Shawn was playing piano. We did everything you're supposed to do in the studio: we left some stuff straight, took some real crazy chances, used a wacky effect just for the hell of it—just tried not to get too dogmatic about what we were doing.

GW: What guitar equipment did you use?

GOSSARD: A Peavey Classic 50-watt head and Peavey cabinet, a '67 Marshall 100-watt bass head, a Gretsch Roundup, a Les Paul, a Big Muff and a Univibe. I plan to use all of that stuff on the next Pearl Jam album, but I'll be experimenting more with them. I'll also be bringing in a lot of smaller amps and screwing around with different effects— I want to be pretty radical as far as getting different sounds.

GW: The bass lines in Brad, unlike in Pearl Jam, tend to lead the charge more than the guitar.

GOSSARD: Yeah, I agree to a certain extent. I think Jeremy is a great pocket bass player, and the two of us developed a real nice dialogue in the studio. It was no problem for me to let my guitar hang back if he wanted to lead the way, and that's something I would like to see more of in Pearl Jam. I'm looking forward to the bass and drums playing much more of a lead role in Pearl Jam. That idea really excites me, as it will open up a whole new world for me as a guitarist. It would be cool to pull against the bass and drums instead of being locked into the rhythm section all the time.

GW: You recorded *Ten* in two months. Will Pearl Jam spend more time on the next album?

GOSSARD: No. We've given ourselves two months, and we plan to get it done in that time. But we plan to do it in a completely different way this time—to record and mix three songs a week until we're done. That way, everyone will be involved until the end, and no one will want to leave because their parts are already done. When you record everything separately, you can run into problems when, for example, the drum tracks are done but the song keeps evolving and the drums can't evolve with the rest of the track unless you totally redo them. So it'll be a two-month record, but I think it'll be more like a two-week record in the way the songs will be recorded quickly. We'll probably record 25 songs by the time we're through.

GW: Have you and Mike [*McCready, Pearl Jam guitarist*] figured out how you will split up the guitar duties on the next album?

GOSSARD: None of that will be worked out until we start rehearsing. We have about 20 songs already written, but our main objective will be to just go in the studio and jam. The first thing we have to do is figure out where the band is collectively, then we'll be able to bring in individual things. Mike and I have both learned a lot in the past year, and I think we're going to shoot for the most challenging guitar arrangements possible.

We plan on utilizing, to the fullest extent, having two guitar players. We each have unique styles, and we want each guitar part to serve some purpose—not just have one guitar double the other's part. That's a standard trap you can fall into with a two-guitar band, and we want to escape that.

GW: How does your style differ from Mike's?

GOSSARD: One of Mike's greatest strengths is that he has the emotive power to just explode and play something totally wild at any time. I, on the other hand, have a tendency to be more of a pocket player—I'm more conscious of the groove or the riff. And both elements are very important for a song that has groove *and* excitement.

GW: Obviously, you have very clear ideas about how you would like to record the next Pearl Jam album. Where does a producer like Brendan O'Brien [*Black Crowes, Red Hot Chili Peppers*] fit in?

GOSSARD: Brendan will be the objective force in the project. It's really good to have an outside perspective when making an album, especially when it's someone you respect. Brendan is a great guitar player, tremendous engineer, and he knows what he's doing in the studio. Hanging out with him is a blast, too. I like the fact that his intentions are purely musical.

GW: Is it strange to be planning the next record when *Ten* is still near the top of the charts?

GOSSARD: We're trying not to live in the past, and *Ten* is already two years old. It's wonderful that the record is still selling so well and that we have nothing to worry about as far as a budget is concerned, but the bottom line is that we're excited about making more music, and *Ten* is certainly not the end of the road for Pearl Jam.

Releasing an album "too soon" is a real record company and marketing way of thinking. To us, the bottom line is that if the music is good, no one will have a problem having too much of it.

Guitar World, February 1995

The Father, the Son, and the Holy Grunge

Soundgarden's Kim Thayil prostrates himself at the altar of the Melvins' Buzz Osbourne, the primeval God of Grunge.

By Jeff Gilbert

THROUGHOUT HISTORY, THERE have been many celebrated instances of the master/disciple relationship. In ancient Greece, Socrates and Plato. On the desert planet of Tatooine, Obi-Wan Kenobi and Luke Skywalker. And in Seattle, the Melvins and Soundgarden.

The *Melvins*? The fact is, the band from Aberdeen, Washington, and their guitarist, Buzz Osbourne, have heavily influenced every Northwest-based band to record since 1985. Nirvana, Mudhoney, Alice in Chains, the Screaming Trees, Pearl Jam—all have readily credited Osbourne and the Melvins with creating the volcanic sludge that came to be tagged grunge.

Osbourne's detuned, creepy-crawly guitar playing has spawned thousands of imitators, some of whom have become rich and famous. Some of whom have made important music. And some of whom still haven't figured out that you can't play Black Sabbath songs in regular tuning.

We enlisted grunge guru Kim Thayil of Soundgarden, who has built a Platinum retirement plan on gargantuan, Melvinian chording, to interview Osbourne. Our goal? To unearth the real origins of grunge and the fabled alternative tunings that have come to characterize heavy guitar rock in the Nineties.

Osbourne enters the room looking eerily like *The Simpsons'* Sideshow Bob, with his "bird nest on steroids" hair, billowy pants, goofy grin and penchant for dishing out quick jokes. Hardly what you'd expect from the man who may well have laid the cornerstone upon which the music of Nirvana, Soundgarden, et al was built.

Thayil sits reverentially nearby, eager to talk about guitars, amps, the Stooges, Kiss, van gigs, and the Melvins' latest album, *Stoner Witch* (Atlantic). Armed with a mere half case of Budweiser, a large pepperoni pizza and a tape recorder loaded with pink bunny Energizers, *Guitar World* played host to this Grunge Summit, exploring the genesis of the hairiest of all guitar sounds.

GUITAR WORLD: Kim, do you remember the first time you saw the Melvins?

KIM THAYIL: I think it was in 1984. The bill was the U-Men and Melvins, and it was at the Mountaineers [*a Seattle mountain club auditorium used for weekend concerts*].

BUZZ OSBOURNE: That was the first relatively sizable show we played in Seattle, actually.

THAYIL: Everyone kept yelling, "Kim, did you hear that?" It was like, "The fuckin' Melvins are slow as hell!" I was blown away—the Melvins went from being the fastest band in town to the slowest. It was a pretty amazing and courageous move. Everyone was trying to be punk rock, a kind of art-damage thing, and the Melvins decided to be the heaviest band in the world.

OSBOURNE: It was the Black Flag thing.

THAYIL: That was right around the time Green River [*Stone Gossard's pre-Pearl Jam band*] and Soundgarden first started getting together. Mark Arm [Mudhoney] and Ben Shepherd [*Soundgarden bassist, but at the time in a punk band called March of Crimes*] and I would always have conversations about the Stooges. We were talking about that "feel," that sort of MC5 stuff when it was a slow, depressing, trippy, heavy thing. We talked about that a lot. But the Melvins went and did it.

OSBOURNE: At that time it seemed like all the bands in Seattle wanted to sound like Aerosmith.

THAYIL: Who? Green River? Not us!

GW: [laughs] Kim, what, for you, was cool about the Melvins?

THAYIL: I thought it was a courageous step for them to go from being really fast to being really slow. That was a big deal to all the punk rock guys, who thought fast meant powerful. Part of the reason that excited me may have been that it appealed to a guilty pleasure of mine, because I've always liked slow, heavy music. So I thought they were doing heavy metal the way metal should be done. People said, "Well, slow is metal; if you slow down, it's not punk." And metal was frowned upon. But the Melvins' music didn't have the operatic vocals and self-indulgent, never-ending guitar solos. Or the boots! [laughs] Those heavy metal boots.

GW: St. Vitus was another band to really slow things down—they were, like, the slowest band in the world—at about the same time. Buzz, did the Melvins come before or after St. Vitus?

OSBOURNE: They put out their first album before we did.

THAYIL: Your first recorded stuff appeared on *Deep Six* [*a seminal Seattle sound compilation on C/Z Records*] in 1985. *Deep Six* was the first recorded documentation of the Seattle scene.

OSBOURNE: Yeah, although when *Deep Six* came out nobody gave a shit about it; nobody bought that album.

GW: Buzz, you guys moved to San Francisco shortly before the "Seattle sound" exploded. Why did you leave Seattle?

OSBOURNE: At the time, we'd played as much as we could and nothing was really happening. In moving, we weren't really leaving much behind. At the time we left Seattle, the most money we'd ever made there was $160; it took us until about the end of '88 to finally break the $200 barrier.

GW: Do you regret having left before everything started kicking in?

OSBOURNE: No. Most of the records we've ever made have come since we moved. I don't think our career suffered at all. I don't know what we would have accomplished here that we didn't eventually end up doing, anyway.

GW: What's amazing is that the records you made after you were gone still continued to influence bands like Soundgarden and Nirvana.

THAYIL: That's right. I think everyone up here still considers the Melvins a Seattle band. You're just kind of displaced.

GW: Even though they've been credited with pioneering the use of the "dropped-D" tuning, Soundgarden have always maintained that it was the Melvins who came up with it. Kim, do you recall when Buzz first showed you that tuning technique?

THAYIL: I remember Buzz and I going to see St. Vitus in around 1986, after which we went back to Mark Arm's apartment. We were spinning records and talking about how Kiss tuned everything to E-flat. Mark and I planned to just drop everything down a half-step, but Buzz said that all you had to do was just drop the E-string down to D. I was like, "Really?" At that point, I played everything in regular tuning. I didn't bother with different tunings because I was having a hard enough time figuring out the regular one. I mean, barre chords were my staple. And then we D-tuned and started experimenting. We've never stopped.

OSBOURNE: It opens up all kinds of new doors.

THAYIL: It was a big change for us, because I suddenly had all these ideas I brought to the band and said, "Look at this! See what Buzz is saying about how to do this? We wouldn't have been able to come up with a riff like that in regular tuning!" We first used it on "Nothing to Say" [Screaming Life, *Sub Pop, 1987*] and "Flower" [Flower EP, *SST, 1988*].

GW: Buzz, how did you develop the "dropped-D"?

OSBOURNE: I learned it from some guy—a metal kid, actually—in Aberdeen. Since I found that out, I've done all different kinds of tunings.

THAYIL: People don't understand that you don't tune to make things more difficult for yourself. Using different tunings isn't to challenge yourself and make you this virtuoso.

OSBOURNE: What amazes me, and I'm sure this happens to you too, Kim, is when I go into some guitar store, those kids in there can play circles around me.

THAYIL: Sure, and they're 15.

OSBOURNE: And those guys will probably never do anything.

THAYIL: They'll probably work on the other end of the counter at Guitar Center, selling guitars and giving lessons. They spend too much time seeing how fast they can play. Maybe they'll end up being a studio guy, because those guys don't like songs; they're into the athleticism of it.

OSBOURNE: That's it. We're not Steve Vai-type guitar players, nothing like that. But we've certainly contributed a lot more musically than all these kids that can play fuckin' "Eruption." I can go into music stores and can be the biggest guitar dummy in there—and the only one who has a record contract. It's insane.

THAYIL: It is, because you're more of an influence on bands than the people who've mastered all the electronics.

OSBOURNE: Take somebody like Kurt Cobain. He was a good songwriter, but he wasn't a guitar virtuoso. He was an average player, but that's not what it's about. There were 13-year-old metal kids who could play circles around him. Just because you're in a successful band, they automatically assume that you're some guitar virtuoso. A lot of kids come up to me and say, "Can you play this?" And I say, "No."

THAYIL: I used to listen to *Sgt. Pepper's* and thought that the Beatles played all the instruments on the record—the French horn, the trumpet, the strings. I said, "Man, I really want to be a rock star, but learning guitar will only be the beginning, because I'll also have to learn French horns, trumpets, piano—and how to write music! Do I have to learn how to write music first before I can even play an instrument?" It was way beyond me. I set this really weird standard for myself that intimidated me for years, and as a result I never picked up a guitar. I'd look at chord charts: C, C7, G7, and go, "What's a sharp? It's one of those numbers they don't have in math but they have in music." [*laughs*]

GW: Kurt Cobain was a loyal disciple of the Melvins.

THAYIL: You were a big influence on Kurt and Nirvana, you influenced us and you had the same influence on Green River, even though they had a hard enough time playing in standard tuning, let alone bothering with dropped-D. They were trying to be Aerosmith, no reason to worry about trying to be like Sabbath.

OSBOURNE: It was haircuts. Just haircuts.

THAYIL: Nirvana and Soundgarden are probably the two biggest bands directly influenced by you. Then other bands were influenced by us. Even Urge Overkill has dropped-D tuned songs now. But it's not just that it's dropped-D, it's the style of playing slower than slow.

GW: Buzz, which is more important to you, the song or the riff? Because dropped-D tunings can help you get amazing riff sounds.

OSBOURNE: I don't know—both, actually. A lot of my favorite songs have no riffs to speak of—they just have drums, bass and vocals. It's hard to say which is more important, the riff or the song, because the riff can become the song; it depends on how good the riff is.

THAYIL: A riff is just another way of describing dynamics. Soundgarden was kind of riff-oriented when we started. The idea was to write really mean riffs, then blow it by adding really pretty parts. We'd think, "Oh, that's killer; run over the bird's nest with a lawn mower!"

GW: Early Soundgarden was all riff.

THAYIL: Earliest recorded Soundgarden. There's a good 30 songs that have never been released that we played live all the time. They were riffy, but not Metallica punk riffy. They had a little bit more of a childlike, Pere Ubu meets Charlie Brown meets Black Sabbath thing.

Buzz, you guys released solo records that spoofed the Kiss solo albums. Is Kiss still one of your favorite bands?

OSBOURNE: I don't listen to Kiss as much as I used to. My favorite band now is ZZ Top. I really like their new record. I still enjoy a lot of that Kiss stuff when I hear it, though.

GW: I was surprised to see that the Melvins weren't included on the *Kiss My Ass* (Mercury) tribute album.

OSBOURNE: Redd Kross isn't on there either, and those guys are the ultimate Kiss tribute band. I don't really know what Gene Simmons' motivation was. Trying to get as many people who have sold records on there as he could so he could sell records, I guess.

GW: Gene was impressed with your solo album spoof. Did he like your version of "Goin' Blind" [*Houdini*]?

OSBOURNE: I'm not quite sure what he thought of it. We told Gene that Kurt Cobain sang on it, which was a lie. Gene's ears perked up more about that song after he heard that.

THAYIL: Is *Hotter than Hell* still your favorite Kiss album?

OSBOURNE: I would have to say yes.

THAYIL: How do you feel about the success of the bands you've influenced? To have been around so long and see them have a certain amount of success... I mean, the guys in Nirvana were practically your little brothers for a little while.

OSBOURNE: I'm not walking around bitter about that stuff, if that's what you mean. Nirvana and Soundgarden are far more commercial-sounding than we are. We're a much harder band to sell, so it doesn't surprise me. It's not like I'm going, "God, I was trying to write 'Teen Spirit' and it just didn't work for me." I've known all the people in both bands for years and I'm really glad that bands who have achieved success say they were influenced by me. It makes me feel like the stuff we were doing actually mattered to somebody.

GW: Has there been any fallout as a result of all this? Any perks?

OSBOURNE: I'd have to be a fool to say that the success of these bands hasn't helped us. It's totally helped us. We've continued, at a slow rate, to sell more records every time we put an album out. When I think about where I was when this band started and what my goals were for us, which was literally to play somewhere cool like the Metropolis [*legendary Seattle punk club*], as compared to what has actually happened, I certainly have to say that I've surpassed my early goals.

THAYIL: The kind of success we're having is a little bit more than the standard that you set for yourself starting out—and it's more than you can expect. I used to say, "Well, I'd like to have a Gold record," but what does that mean? Nothing. There's no standard to measure that by. Maybe it's a milestone, but does it mean our TVs get bigger?

Do we get more beer?

OSBOURNE: Yes, actually. [*laughs*]

THAYIL: Oh, yeah.

GW: One fallout of success is having products named after you. Buzz, weren't you a consultant on a foot pedal design that used your name?

THAYIL: It wasn't the DOD Grunge Pedal, was it? Have you seen that? The inside of the accompanying booklet says: "How to get the Melvins sound; how to get the Accused sound." I bought the thing, not to use it, but simply as a souvenir.

GW: I remember you saying, "Great, I just bought a pedal to make me sound like me." [*everyone laughs*]

OSBOURNE: It's called the Buzz Box, and it is put out by DOD. I had nothing to do with it. I mean, does my guitar really sound that bad? [*laughs*] The guys at DOD are kind of crazy; I have to give them credit for that. A guy there was always bugging me at shows about how we got the sound on the *Eggnog* record. I used this thing called a Blue Box, an octave divider from the early Seventies. So this guy says, "I want to design a pedal; we'll call it the Buzz Box and get that sound out of it." But it wasn't so much that he wanted to do an endorsement or anything. I think he just liked the sound of it. So he came to one of our shows and looked inside the Blue Box. He kind of duplicated it and combined it with the Grunge Pedal in a new pedal. When I heard it, it was just atrocious! So I thought, "These people don't really have a deal with me, and this thing is pretty much worthless; yes, I think I can get behind this product!" [*laughs*] I have to admire DOD for putting out something that insane. Yes, the Buzz Box is totally worthless. It sounds like a vacuum cleaner. [*laughs*]

I ended up using it on a few noise things on *Stoner Witch*, but the record that we used it on most was one that came out before *Stoner Witch* called *Prick*, a total noise crap record we did just for the weirdness factor alone. Complete and utter nonsense, a total joke. We've taken a lot of shit for it, too. I would say it has no redeeming social value whatsoever and is easily the stupidest record we've ever done. There's something to be said for that.

THAYIL: How many albums have you released?

OSBOURNE: There's *Gluey Porch Treatments* [*Alchemy Records, 1987*]; *Ozma* [*Boner Records, 1989*]; *Bullhead* [*Boner Records, 1990*]; *Eggnog* [*10-inch EP, Boner Records, 1986*]; the solo albums [Dale, King Buzzo, Joe, all *Boner Records 1992*], and then one called *Lysol*, which we changed to *Self-Titled* [*Boner Records, 1992*]. C/Z Records reissued our first 7-inch single [*untitled, 1986*] album length with extra songs on it. Then *Houdini* [*Atlantic Records, 1993*], a *German Live Melvins* [*import, label unknown*], *Prick* [*released under the name* Snivlem, *Amphetamine Reptile, 1994*], and *Stoner Witch* [*Atlantic Records, 1994*].

THAYIL: Is *Prick* comparable to Lou Reed's *Metal Machine Music?*

OSBOURNE: It's not that serious; it's far stupider. It was the perfect record to put out between two major label releases. Atlantic Records freaked out before they heard the record. "You guys wanna do what? Put out a record on an independent? That's bullshit! You guys have a contract with us!" We said, "Why don't you guys just listen to it, because you're not going to be interested." The European division of the label freaked out, too, and they hadn't heard it either. Finally, we didn't hear a word about it, and they let us put it out. *Prick* sold about 10,000 copies or something. I would have been happy if it had sold two. 10,000? My heart almost stopped. We're taking the money we made from it and applying it to the advance we got for our new album.

THAYIL: Would you describe your fans as coming from more of a metal camp than a punk rock camp?

OSBOURNE: It's varied.

THAYIL: What do you top out at, sales-wise?

OSBOURNE: About 70,000. The most we could do on an independent was 25,000.

THAYIL: Kurt Cobain produced *Houdini*. Were you happy with the way that came out?

OSBOURNE: I wish we could have done more. The guy that we just worked with, GGGarth Richardson [*Red Hot Chili Peppers, Rage Against the Machine, L7*] was great. That's the first time we've really worked with a producer in the classical sense.

GW: How was it different working with Kurt?

OSBOURNE: The difference is Kurt wasn't a producer. What I was looking for from Kurt was musical input, not knob-twiddling input. I was burnt out at the time, and thought another creative collaborator would help out. But it didn't really happen. Dale [*Crover, Melvins drummer*] and I did most of that album ourselves.

GW: *Stoner Witch* is less accessible than *Houdini*.

OSBOURNE: I think it's more accessible.

GW: I'm referring particularly to side two. Side one reinterprets the metal/punk/grunge thing and has some really cool songs and riffs. On side two, however, you seem to be taking chances with all that free-form guitar jizz. Did the label offer any kind of resistance about that?

OSBOURNE: The reason side two is stacked up with weird tunes is because we wanted people to make it through the stuff they might be able to latch onto, and ease them into the weird part of the record.

THAYIL: You make records pretty quickly; this one was done in 19 days. Do you think if you spent more time making a record, you might get more out of it?

OSBOURNE: Maybe. I don't know. This was the longest time we ever stayed in one studio, actually. The only real problem with *Houdini* for me is we weren't really a whole band, and I think it kind of sounded like that. We've got the strongest live lineup we've ever had now. The band sounds good. It doesn't sound like it did in '86.

GW: When you guys opened up for Soundgarden at the Paramount here in Seattle at the end of their *Badmotorfinger* tour, you made what I considered a pretty ballsy move: coming out after a booming introduction—"Ladies and gentlemen...the Melvins!"—and just playing one note as slowly as humanly possible.

OSBOURNE: That was because the review of the show the night before said that we basically just played one note the whole night.

GW: And you did, for about 15 minutes. A lot of the jocks in the crowd didn't get it.

THAYIL: Speaking of those jocks, some of our friends were riding us. They said, "You guys used to be cool, but now look at your audience—a bunch of goobers."

GW: That wasn't your audience, it was MTV's.

OSBOURNE: It doesn't matter. I mean, I just went and saw ZZ Top, and it was one of the most white-trash, scary audiences I've ever seen, and those guys played an amazing show, nevertheless. That's their job.

GW: Would you like to tour with ZZ Top?

OSBOURNE: I would not like to tour for their audience, but I would like to tour with them. It would be great, but their audience is very, very scary. If you could stack up all the warrants that were due in that crowd...Jesus!

GW: Are you happy with the way things are going for the Melvins?

OSBOURNE: I don't really know. I mean, I've been doing this for 10 years. Most bands don't even make it for 10 months. Hopefully, this is the last lineup we're going to have. We have no intention of stopping or quitting. I don't know what else I'd do. I don't even know if we've made our best record yet.

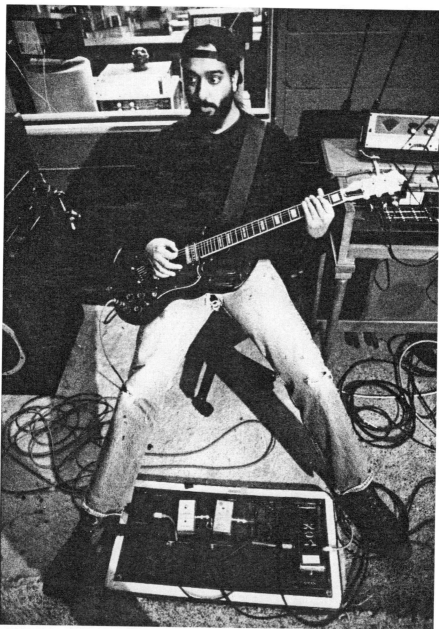

KIM THAYIL of SOUNDGARDEN

Guitar World, December 1995

Heavy Mettle

Soundgarden may excel at playing devastatingly heavy riffs—but don't call them metal. Guitarist Kim Thayil explains.

By Jeff Gilbert

F IT'S LOUD and has lots of noisy guitars, uncombed hair and untucked T-shirts, it must be metal, right? Soundgarden know this better than most. One of rock's premier alternative groups, they keep getting nominated for (and winning) embarrassing awards like "Best Metal Band," "Best Metal Song" and "Best Metal Video." Not surprisingly, this phenomenon has not thrilled the band, which began its career far from the metal mainstream on the then-fledgling indie label, Sub Pop.

"In the beginning, our fans came from the punk rock crowd," says guitarist Kim Thayil. "They abandoned us when they thought we had sold out the punk tenets, getting on a major label and touring with Guns N' Roses. "There were fashion issues and social issues, and people thought we no longer belonged to their scene, to their particular sub-culture."

That Soundgarden is associated with the metal genre isn't altogether surprising, of course, considering the fact that their six-album, 11-year legacy has been soldered with dirge-like guitar riffs at volumes reserved for heavy machinery and wrecking balls. But while "heavy" is something Thayil has always craved, "metal" and its low-brow trappings are not. "Back when I was in school, your *heavier* metal things like Judas Priest started coming out," he recalls. "I thought it was kind of goony and not particularly smart. It wasn't witty. The Stooges are heavier and scarier than any of that shit."

GUITAR WORLD: You've often cited Kiss' Ace Frehley as a prime guitar influence. Why didn't you follow him, as many others did, down the path to heavy metal?

KIM THAYIL: Because Kiss wasn't very smart music. The metal thing tended to be a bit sexist and sophomoric and racist and just kinda dopey. I may not be very social, or socially graceful, but fuck it, I was smarter than the guys who were into metal. I just liked listening to rock and playing guitar and reading a lot. Guitar and books, that was it.

GW: So you found alternative rock's relatively literate esthetic to be attractive?

THAYIL: Precisely. Alternative rock bands involved themselves politically and drew from literary and film sources, whereas metalists drew from rock or teenage experiences. But I was also drawn to the fact that it was loud. The vocals were loud, it was aggressive, fast and heavy; It just seemed to be like me.

GW: Was there a particular concert you saw that you'd classify as life-altering?

THAYIL: Not really. I didn't go to a concert until I was 18 or 19—the first one I saw was David Bowie. The next one I saw was the Ramones. I went to see Devo during their yellow jumpsuit phase. Their gimmick was attractive. They seemed smart and dark and cynical.

Devo was for smart kids in school. A lot of those kids weren't into Kiss and they were hesitant to get into punk rock, but they got into Devo. And the next thing was Elvis Costello. The coolest rock bands are those which are influenced by poetry or movies.

GW: What does "technique" mean to you? Can technique be differentiated from style?

THAYIL: Your lack of technique can be part of your style. The thing about style is that it's more entertaining, more important and hopefully more intellectual than technique. To me technique means proficiency.

Every so often Soundgarden writes songs that are beyond our ability. The idea is not to make things tough on yourself. Sure that's a challenge, but it's kind of foolish and dumb. Tools are there to make it easier to express your ideas. You don't go and try to hammer a nail with a sponge or a basketball. Get a good hammer! People waste their time. The reason people use alternate tunings is to make slide guitar easier or to make playing a certain chord easier.

GW: When were you aware that you were working outside of the mainstream, not that you ever worked in the mainstream?

THAYIL: Yeah, I don't think I ever did. The first year I played guitar I was trying to play faster than Hendrix. Speed was the whole thing. You had to be able to play really fast, which is a really immature, sophomoric approach to music or your instrument.

GW: Don't you think you had to go through that to get where you are now?

THAYIL: I still do that; it's a nervous habit. I just play really fast. I know it's a dumb thing to do and it's annoying. I should just slow down.

GW: Was there a moment when you were learning your instrument where you experienced a proficiency breakthrough?

THAYIL: I wasn't interested so much in playing guitar as in having the guitar facilitate writing guitar riffs. There was a time, though, when I realized that as you move a barre chord up and down the neck, you're changing the key.

That was a big deal, but I think my biggest breakthrough came when I started playing lead. I went about it in a weird way, memorizing the entire neck in the key of A. Then I memorized it in the key of C. Then in D. I memorized all the notes out of patterns. I was out of my mind. Then I started learning modalities as this visual relationship between barre chords on the neck. I ended up forgetting all the modalities because I play more by ear. At this point I couldn't watch my fingers and think what mode I'm playing in. I just don't give a shit anymore.

GW: Now that you've sold millions of records, do you still consider Soundgarden to be an "alternative" band?

THAYIL: Over the past four years, the world has conformed to fit us, and for all intents and purposes, our brand of "alternative" music has entered the mainstream.

People perceived the rock world as a dichotomy: "metal versus alternative" or "mainstream versus underground." Dichotomies aren't real, they're human constructs. Cat is not the opposite of dog. Anti-dog is the opposite of dog. It's stupid and naive to ask, "Are you metal or alternative?" They're holding on to these standards, and they really don't exist. Come on, man. Buy a fuckin' Ramones record; get an education!

ALICE IN CHAINS

Guitar World, January 1996

Go Ask Alice

Jerry Cantrell offers some entertaining and frank observations on the state of Alice in Chains, the glories of the band's new, self-titled album, and life in the Seattle wonderland.

By Jeff Gilbert

WHILE SEATTLE HAS certainly enjoyed its 15 minutes of fame as "the capital of grunge," the city has also paid a heavy price for its rock and roll notoriety. A recent newspaper headline proclaimed it "Drug Town, U.S.A.," while a noted music critic estimated that "one in four Seattle musicians is involved with heroin." *Rolling Stone* even went so far as to wryly note that heroin was "back on the charts," and that Seattle, along with New York and Hollywood, was a hot spot for the drug.

While claims that Seattle is a heroin mecca may be exaggerated, there is more than a grain of truth to the rumors and media assertions about the drug's prevalence in the city. One can only assume that the high profile overdoses of Mother Love Bone's Andrew Wood, Seven Year Bitch's Stephanie Sargent, and Hole's Kristen Pfaff are but the most visible manifestations of the drug's impact on the local music scene.

Among the most highly publicized, long-term drug sagas has been that of Alice in Chains vocalist Layne Staley, whose on-again/off-again involvement with heroin has sometimes attracted nearly as much attention as the band's music. "Alice in Chains' videos are elegant little travelogues of junkie life," wrote *Spin* magazine in March of 1995. "Heroin addicts and struggling former addicts hear something in Layne's grade-school junkie poetry, a kind of siren." Plagued by persistent reports that they had been torn apart by drug-related internal stress, haunted by morbid death-pool predictions that consistently pick Staley as Seattle's "most likely to O.D.," stymied by Staley's recent collaboration with Pearl Jam guitarist Mike McCready in Mad Season, and hampered by an apparent inability to make it to prestigious gigs like Woodstock '94 and the Rock and Roll Hall of Fame grand opening, Alice in Chains responded with a self-imposed media silence.

"We made one final statement to the press when we decided to break the lines of communication," says guitarist Jerry Cantrell. "We were a fucking overloaded sponge that needed to be wrung out. We seriously needed the time to sit down and start fresh. That's what we did."

He pauses before adding, "We're definitely not perfect people, but I'm not apologizing for shit. I'm doing the best I can with what I got and that's all anybody in my band is doing."

Except for talk specifically related to the new record, the band's vow of silence remains unbroken. Cantrell refuses to discuss any of Alice in Chains' past or present problems or comment on Staley's drug use, but is happy to talk about the group's new self-titled album. Building on the exquisitely sinister, squalid self-loathing that permeated *Dirt*, which many critics hailed as the drug album of the Nineties, Cantrell and company have forged their most darkly introspective work to date. From the magnificent black walls of guitar riffery that propel "Grind" and "Sludge Factory," to the lush, kaleidoscopic harmonies of "Heaven Beside You" and "Frogs," *Alice in Chains* finds the band once again scraping the bottom of their psychic barrels to emerge at the top of their musical game. As Cantrell enthusiastically remarks, it's a "fuckin' dangerous record."

GUITAR WORLD: Does Alice in Chains plan to tour in support of this album?

JERRY CANTRELL: Absolutely. I'm so anxious to get back out on the road. We worked on this record for six months, so completing it was a big monkey to get off our backs. I don't mind saying that it feels real good to be done with it. It was really hard to stay focused with all of the rumors flying around. You can say, "Fuck you, you don't know what's up" to people as many times as you want, but it still hurts. We've taken some ragging. It's the "kids on the playground" thing: "Those kids are calling me names. What am I gonna do? Am I gonna cry? Am I gonna lower myself to their level and fight them? Or am I gonna say 'Fuck you' and walk away?" We walked away and did our own thing. That's what the record is. We learned to survive on the playground. You can't lower yourself to their level and you can't let them get to you. Because at the end of the day, they'll be the guys working at McDonald's with bald heads and five kids and three ex-wives hollering for child support.

GW: When Alice in Chains dropped off the Metallica tour in 1994, it generated a lot of speculation about the band's future.

CANTRELL: Actually, the speculation started before that, with the lyrics on *Dirt*. That was the beginning of it all. That's a hard record.

GW: The new one is hard, too.

CANTRELL: Yeah, this record is also lyrically hard. I can't say one record is better than the other, but this one is a lot more tongue-in-cheek. It has a lot more irony.

GW: The first line on the album is, "In your darkest hole, you'd be well-advised not to plan my funeral before the body dies." That seems to set the tone for the entire record and fire one back at the rumor mill.

CANTRELL: You're right; it pretty much says it all right there.

GW: After leaving the Metallica tour, you also dropped out of Woodstock '94 and then recently canceled your appearance at the Rock and Roll Hall of Fame grand opening concert.

CANTRELL: The Rock and Roll Hall of Fame concert came in the middle of us making this record. We really didn't have the luxury to go out and do it. It's unfortunate we missed gigs that people wanted to see us play. That's the thing that pisses me off the most. I take responsibility for that as much as anyone. But shit happens. What are you gonna do?

GW: Is that the official line then?

CANTRELL: Look. People have been saying we're over since *Dirt*. And people will say now that this is our last record and that we'll never tour again. Go ahead and think that. We're the kind of band that has always been able to do the opposite of what people expect.

GW: The media has a tendency to find a weak link and keep hammering on it until it breaks.

CANTRELL: Totally. They'll pick on a sore spot until it's an infected scab. Hey, if you want to keep licking, that's cool, but I don't have to let you pick my scabs. I pick my own. [*laughs*] It's hard not to give people like that power.

At the end of the day, we've done an incredible job, have great fans, and awesome people around us. The band sticks together because we're a tight bunch of friends. We've got that "in the trenches" vibe. Nobody knows what the fuck that's about except for your buddy right across from you.

I'll tell you, the whole experience has been interesting, and I wouldn't have it any other way. I've lived some of the most incredible moments and had some of the most insane adventures of my life—and I'm only 29 years old. It blows me away sometimes. I feel so thankful for my experiences. Hold on—I think I'm gonna cry. [*laughs*]

GW: How has your outlook on life evolved since the band took off?

CANTRELL: I think I ended up right back where I always was. Sometimes you have to completely lose yourself to find yourself. There were times in the last year and a half where I didn't even want to play anymore. Or, at least, I thought I didn't want to play. All of the baggage and bullshit that comes along with it didn't seem to be offset by the music we created. I finally slapped some sense into my head and realized that you couldn't ask for anything better than the work we've done and the people we've been fortunate enough to play for. Our fans are almost as die-hard and tough as we are. To take that for granted would be a sad thing. But at the same time you have to be a human being. When you hurt and it's time to rest, you have to sit down, chill out, and hope you can come back swinging.

GW: Overall, has the band's success had a positive or negative impact on you?

CANTRELL: It's been positive to me, man. I own my own home, I can feed myself, I can enjoy it with my friends...

GW: Those are certainly the financial rewards, but what about artistically?

CANTRELL: Artistically, I'm fine. Success has a lot to do with luck, but it also involves a lot of real hard work. The thing about success is you really can't gauge things by album sales. Of course, I want to sell as many records as I can, but that's not why I do it. You finish a record because you think it's fucking good. We wouldn't be putting records out if we didn't think we were topping ourselves each time. I say that with confidence. I hope I don't come off sounding like a braggart, but it's good shit. There's other great shit out there, but I think we're right up there with the best of them.

GW: Let's talk about your new album. Wasn't this originally intended to be your solo record?

CANTRELL: No, though there are two songs, "Grind" and "Again," that ended up being on this album, that came from the demo project which I was halfheartedly working on while Layne was doing the Mad Season sessions. To be honest, I'm too much of a sentimental fuck; I don't want to play with another band. I didn't feel I could put something else out that could top what Alice in Chains could do together.

GW: One of the great things about a new Alice in Chains record is that you never know what it's going to sound like.

CANTRELL: We've been really good with the element of surprise. We're a tight bunch of guys. Even now that we live apart and have our own places, that musical tightness never leaves. The most fun thing about this band is that I never know where the fuck we're gonna end up. None of the other guys do, either. [*laughs*] We stand back and go, "Wow, how did we do that?"

GW: Do you still consider Alice in Chains to be a "heavy metal" band or are you just "rock" now?

CANTRELL: No, we're part of the metal thing. We're a lot of different things, too. I don't quite know what the mixture is, but there's definitely metal, blues, rock and roll, maybe a touch of punk. The metal part will never leave us—and I never want it to.

GW: Coming from a metal and hard rock background, do you mourn metal's passing?

CANTRELL: No, not at all. One thing I've learned about our band is that you never count anything out, ever. Because when you do, it usually snaps right back up and pops you in the face. As far as the passing of metal goes, we're part metal and we're still around. It's a very cyclical progression; rap had that big cycle, the Seattle bands had that cycle, now the pop-punk thing is having its cycle. But the fact is there are still plenty of metal bands out there.

GW: Metal bands today seem in disarray. It strikes me that they're totally obsessed with making things heavy, at the expense of creativity or originality.

CANTRELL: I've always been interested in bands that make heavy shit without sounding overtly heavy. There's something about having strength and not flaunting it. It's not about coming out and mauling your ass, but easing in. Before you know it, you're in a death lock, which you didn't see coming because it was so smooth and seductive you didn't know it until it had your face down on the canvas. I'm always intrigued by that. To me, being heavy has nothing to do with how many speakers you blow or how many decibels you play at.

GW: The type of material you're writing now is light years ahead of where you began, as a riff-based metal band. Have you thought about what contributed to that progression?

CANTRELL: I think the longer you stick with something, the better you're going to get at it. I'm going to keep thinking about topping myself every time. I can say very confidently that Alice in Chains has done that on every record. It surprises me. I don't go in there expecting that, but I do go in there hoping for it.

GW: Does everybody in the band write?

CANTRELL: Yeah, everybody. We have shared tastes as well as shared dislikes. It's an unspoken language that we have. That's not to say that we don't sometimes disagree on stuff. There have been plenty of times where I think something is completely horrid and the other guys will make me check it out again. For weeks I'll be like, "God, that sucks!" Then one day it's like, "Ohhh, I get it. Okay. That's good!" [*laughs*]

GW: Did that happen to you while you were putting the new album together?

CANTRELL: I thought the solo on "Hate to Feel" was a piece of shit. And the solo on "Grind," for that matter, which is lifted off the ADAT demo I did for the album, works fine. That was the first take I did when I recorded the song. I didn't think it was that strong, but I never got around to fixing it. Toby [*Wright, the band's producer*] kept trying to sell me on it. I kept telling him I wanted to do it better because it just didn't seem to work for me. In the end, it's perfect for the record, but it took me a long time to feel comfortable with it.

GW: So you do the bulk of the songwriting?

CANTRELL: [*tentatively*] Yeah, but that's a pretty misleading statement.

GW: Are you the catalyst, then?

CANTRELL: I wouldn't say that either. [*Bassist*] Mike Inez adds a whole lot to the mix, as well. But I'd say the place where 70 percent of the songs start is with me and Sean [Kinney, drummer]. I'll start a riff, he'll start banging away, and before you know it we're somewhere we didn't expect to be. Without him to bounce shit off of and lead me—and me to lead him when we're both unconscious [*laughs*]—it'd be real hard for me to play. Nobody plays like him. I think the great thing about Sean is that he's got a great sense of humor and isn't full of himself. The fact is he's just a fuckin' Class A, monster player.

GW: You've developed your songwriting skills into a sturdy pop craft without sacrificing the heaviness. Was that an influence from touring with and becoming friends with Van Halen, a band which evolved similarly?

CANTRELL: I wouldn't necessarily pick Van Halen. But on this record I did something that started to scare me for a while. I started to really hear a lot of other influences from my youth. They really started to flow freely. I'd go, "Okay, that sounds like Brian May," or "that sounds like Eddie." There's a riff on the end of "Frogs" that, thanks to that Roto-vibe, reminds me of [Robin Trower's] "Bridge of Sighs." To date, this record probably offers the clearest view of my influences. I could point out 50 of them, from Brian May to Lindsay Buckingham, Davey Johnstone to Hendrix, Iommi to Page; there's all kinds of shit in there. There's some riffs that are pretty obvious. I have to admit that I started to feel really weird when that began happening.

GW: It freaked you out?

CANTRELL: It did, but it felt so natural that I didn't let myself worry about it. We're pretty self-correcting as far as what is right for us. There's not a lot of fucking around.

GW: The guitar solos on this album are shorter and more abstract than your past work, as if you're reaching for something other than the standard "been there, done that, bought a shirt" lead break.

CANTRELL: I've never been a big soloist; I just put in what needs to be there. I'm more of a rhythm player who plays lead—or tries to play lead. I'm not saying I do bad shit, but I just do what fits the part. I'm more interested in what the whole picture is instead of creating a big vehicle for Cantrell to wank off all over everybody.

GW: Your guitar tone on this album is huge. What's your recipe for monster tone?

CANTRELL: My guitar tech, Darrell Peters, is my right-hand man. He's the brains of the outfit, and I'm just the body! I have a basic tone, and if I can verbalize to Darrell what changes I want, he'll get it. Even if what I'm saying makes no sense, he usually knows what I mean and will find what I'm looking for.

My basic set-up, which we used on almost every song, consists of a Bogner Fish preamp and my main G&L Rampage guitar. I also used a Les Paul through a Peavey 5150 amp. Ed [Van Halen] gave me three stacks after we did the tour with him a few years ago. He'd just come out with his new Music Man guitar and the 5150 heads, and I asked him if I could maybe buy one off him. When I came back home after the tour, there were three stacks waiting for me in the fucking garage! [*laughs*] The guy was totally fucking cool! Plus, he gave me a couple of his guitars, too.

GW: Nice guy.

CANTRELL: Super kind. And at the time, I was living in the basement of our manager Kelly Curtis' house, so it was completely full of gear! By the time I got back there, there wasn't even room for me in there!

GW: How many tracks of rhythm guitar do you usually stack up on a given track?

CANTRELL: I always record one rhythm guitar on the left, one on the right, and a lead track up the middle. I've been hard-panning the rhythm guitars like that for a long time.

GW: Do you ever overdub additional guitar parts just to add incidental sounds and textures?

CANTRELL: No, I pretty much just stick to two rhythm guitars panned hard left and right, with a solo track up the middle. Any additional feedback noises or guitar sounds come from those three guitars. People always ask me, "How do you re-create all of the different guitar parts live?" Well, it's never actually a problem, because I always make sure the first guitar part can stand on its own when I play the song live.

As far as the second track of guitars goes, I'll record a single complete track from the beginning of the song to the end, and for that I'll go by feel: I'll get feedback here, or some harmonics there, and that way it'll be different from any other track I'll put down. When we put the tracks together, they usually fit so well that we can fade either one in and out. I cut each new track without thinking about the other one.

GW: Do you work out any of your solos?

CANTRELL: I used to; I'd sit down and really work out something for each tune. Now, I don't think about it at all, and I feel that approach works a lot better for me. Generally, I can't tell people exactly what I played because I don't even know myself!

GW: Would you say that part of your overall approach to recording is to take chances while the tape is rolling, just to see what will happen?

CANTRELL: That's definitely the Alice in Chains way. It's a whole lot of not thinking about it, and a whole lot of just doing it—and making sure the tape is *always* rolling. We had tape running constantly. Even if we didn't have two-inch tape running, we had DATs running constantly. We have so many DATs of so much shit that didn't get used; we have bibles full of outtakes! Maybe we'll release some of the stuff some day. When I was a kid, I always liked outtake records and bootlegs where you could hear little fuck-ups and the guys in the bands talking between the tunes. I thought that was the coolest stuff; it let you in on their vibe. You felt like you were in with the club.

GW: I've often heard you talk about Layne's studio prowess.

CANTRELL: Layne is amazing. We'd go in the back and play football while he was doing vocal tracks. We'd come back and he'd have five awesome-sounding vocal tracks cut. Toby would listen to it and say, "I couldn't have told you to do anything differently."

GW: Speaking of Layne, what do you think of *Above* (Columbia), the Mad Season album ?

CANTRELL: I think it's fucking great. I totally have to 'fess up—I was jealous as shit when I first heard it. It's like somebody taking your girlfriend out. [*laughs*] But after that initial reaction, I went and saw them play at the Moore Theater and I was so proud, I was beaming for them. I almost started crying while I was watching them because it was so cool. Then I felt pissed again because I wasn't up there playing! [*laughs*] I talked to Layne a lot about the record. It was good for him because it blew a bunch of shit out of his head. I've been credited for being a writer and putting out a lot of material with this band and stuff, so I think it was real healthy for him to be able to do that. I have nothing but the greatest respect for the guy. And that record's very soulful. There are some real low, cobwebby passages on that fucker that are cool as fuck. Layne has the most beautiful way of saying something horrible I've ever heard.

Guitar World, July 1996

Soiled Again!

Soundgarden returns to its grungy roots with the devastatingly dirty *Down on the Upside*.

By Alan di Perna

T HE FIRST REALLY nice spring day of the year is always a gift from the gods—especially in rainy, gloomy Seattle. So Kim Thayil can be excused for arriving well past the appointed time for a round of interviews in his manager's office. Soundgarden's intense-eyed blackbeard of a lead guitarist has the leisurely air of a man who's just finished a big job and deserves to kick back for a while. The band's fifth album, *Down on the Upside* (A&M), has just been completed. A sprawling, 16-song opus, it marks a return to the Seattle quartet's raw origins. Which is to say it is less produced than Soundgarden's massive 1994 hit, *Superunknown*. The chunky guitar quotient is way up high, and singer Chris Cornell's "Burton Cummings-esque" arena rock wail is in top form. On the other hand, several of the tunes' song structures have an open-ended quality reminiscent of the more experimental strain of Soundgarden's work on *Superunknown*. This time, the band produced itself, with an assist from engineer Adam Kasper, a friend of the group who also worked on *Superunknown*. Thayil pronounces himself pleased with the result.

"Everyone in the band is really excited right now. The album's completed. That's usually a period of time when everyone's like,

'Wow, all right.' "

With their album fully birthed, Thayil, Cornell, bassist Ben Shepard and drummer Matt Cameron are now turning their attention to the usual round of post-release activities. These include a stint co-headlining this year's Lollapalooza with Metallica—Soundgarden also played Lollapalooza in '92—and a video for the album's first single, "Pretty Noose," directed by popular alterno-cartoonist Frank Kozik.

"It should be a trip," says Thayil. "Hopefully something pretty cool and unique-looking. I think he's gonna do some animation and stuff."

It's been just over a decade since Soundgarden first appeared on the scene, with a track on the influential 1986 *Deep Six* compilation, which also included songs by the Melvins, Green River, Malfunction, the U-Men and Skin Yard. "That album came out before Sub Pop got started," notes Thayil proudly. "So it's *the* cornerstone album of the Seattle scene."

Since that portentous debut, Soundgarden has gone on to define the "heavy alternative" sound of the Nineties. But they've always resolutely resisted categorization. And their fiercely individualistic, hirsute lead guitar man refuses to be taken on any terms other than his own.

GUITAR WORLD: Are you comfortable having the "A-word" [*alternative*] applied to Soundgarden?

KIM THAYIL: There was a time when we preferred it to being called heavy metal. We didn't consider ourselves a heavy metal band, not like the ones that were around in the late Eighties. But for convenience sake, record companies would market us that way. Back then, there wasn't a huge alternative market like there is now, and heavy metal was a big-selling thing. So they'd say, "Well, Soundgarden is heavy metal," though that was probably an error. Then again, I don't think we were very comfortable with the "alternative" tag either.

GW: Do you regard the 1992 Lollapalooza tour as the catalyst for Soundgarden's re-categorization from heavy metal to alternative?

THAYIL: I don't know if it was Lollapalooza. When Nirvana and Pearl

Jam had their success, all of a sudden there was a market for what was considered alternative. Money could be made from putting out bands like that. So all of a sudden people were more inclined to label us "alternative." I don't know. I think it's all just to make things easier for the people who work at record companies and magazines. They all have a target demographic. They all have to be concerned with who their audience is and what their product is. So they're the ones who use the labels, out of convenience for themselves.

GW: Early on, Soundgarden toured with overtly metal acts like Skid Row and Guns N' Roses. What was that like?

THAYIL: It was kind of fun.

GW: Did you get along with those guys?

THAYIL: Yeah. I still occasionally see Duff [McKagan] or Slash when I'm in L.A. or when they're up here in Seattle. Duff lives here, you know. When we're in town, we'll play in their side bands or go see them. And with Skid Row, I still occasionally call [*guitarist Dave*] Snake [Sabo], although I haven't actually spoken to him in a couple of years. And we all got along with Sebastian Bach. He's a really quick-witted, funny guy.

The reason we toured with those bands at that point in time was that there was no band bigger than us doing what we were doing. If we were going to take the opportunity to go on a bigger tour, it looked like the only rock bands out there who were doing well and who we had any degree of respect for were Guns N' Roses and Skid Row. There weren't the Nirvanas or Pearl Jams or anything. At that point, we were the biggest sort of alternative hard rock band coming out. Prior to that, we had toured with bands that were more suited to us, like Faith No More, Voivod, Corrosion of Conformity and Bullet La Volta. But we reached a point where we were able to tour with bigger bands, so we chose to go with Guns N' Roses.

For a long time, we were very interested in touring with Metallica, even back then. That's why we're taking this year's Lollapalooza tour—not because we were interested in doing Lollapalooza again, but because we were interested in touring with Metallica.

GW: What do you expect this year's Lollapalooza is going to be like?

THAYIL: Oh, I think it's pretty much going to be a Metallica/Soundgarden tour. We also have the Ramones and Rancid on the bill. And Screaming Trees, as well.

GW: I heard that all of the bands were Metallica's choice.

THAYIL: That's not really true. We really pushed for the Ramones.

GW: Are you friendly with the Ramones?

THAYIL: Yeah. We toured Australia together and enjoyed each other's company. I know those guys were planning on retiring, but we talked them into doing this.

GW: So tell me, is grunge dead?

THAYIL: Gee, I don't know if it was ever alive. Once again, that's another convenient marketing label that aided the media.

GW: Okay, say the media decides that this thing they've invented called grunge is now dead. How might that affect Soundgarden's future?

THAYIL: Uh, I don't know. I think we're independent of that label. I suppose we're associated with it because we're from Seattle. There's a fraternal thing we have with those other bands that are considered grunge—we're kind of buddies with them and we all grew up together. But I don't think we ever tried for that tag. So if that ship sinks, we're not going down with it.

GW: Was your look inspired by the Zig Zag rolling paper man?

THAYIL: [*laughs*]

GW: Or any member of the Fugs?

THAYIL: No. Not Ginsberg. [*American beat poet Allen Ginsberg frequently performed with Sixties underground group the Fugs.*] But the funny thing is, eight or nine years ago, before Ben joined our band, when he was a bit younger, he and his friends would come see Soundgarden play. And he said his friends called me the Zig Zag man.

GW: There is an uncanny resemblance.

THAYIL: I always thought the Zig Zag man was either North African or Algerian. Isn't Zig Zag a French rolling paper company? That would explain the French Algerian connection. The Zig Zag guy kind of looks Algerian.

GW: What's your favorite track on the new Soundgarden album?

THAYIL: I like "Burden in My Hand," and I like "Never the Machine Forever." There's an earlier mix of "Applebite" that I really liked. I like "Rhinosaur" and "An Unkind." I like "Boot Camp," too.

GW: Where did you record the album?

THAYIL: At Studio Litho and Bad Animals—both here in Seattle. [*Studio Litho was built by Stone Gossard of Pearl Jam. Bad Animals was built by Anne and Nancy Wilson of Heart.*]

GW: Did you have any extra material that didn't make it onto the album?

THAYIL: Yeah. There are a couple of songs that we didn't put on the record. And there's a lot of material that wasn't completed and therefore didn't make the record.

GW: Why did you decide to produce this album yourselves?

THAYIL: Producers are more for singer/songwriters who don't have a band of their own. Or for dancers or models who make videos and sell records. They might need producers to write and arrange music for them. But most rock bands who write their own songs already know how they should sound. We just wanted to make this album a little more natural-sounding—not as overproduced as *Superunknown*.

As we worked on the album we discovered there were other benefits to producing ourselves. For example, we came away with a new sense of "bandness"—a renewed feeling of sharing objectives and goals and solidifying our social and professional roles within the group structure. It's like we went on a survival retreat and got to know each other all over again. It made us deal with being self-governing; to be driving the car rather than sitting in the back seat.

GW: What were the main guitars and amps you used for the *Down on the Upside* sessions?

THAYIL: I used my Guild S-100 a lot, and occasionally a Les Paul. There are lots of Telecasters and Jazzmasters, too. And the amps varied from Marshalls and Mesa/Boogies to Princetons and Fender something-or-others that were the size of radios.

GW: That's interesting. One thinks of you as a big-amp kind of guy.

THAYIL: Yeah. But the nature of this album and the variety among our songs lend themselves to using dinky amps. That's what worked best on songs like "Applebite" and "Blow Up the Outside World."

GW: Did you do that dinky amp bit on *Superunknown* at all?

THAYIL: Maybe a little bit, yeah. I think there were Fender Twins and stuff.

GW: Is that a real Leslie cabinet on "Black Hole Sun"?

THAYIL: Yes.

GW: That sound on the intro to "Pretty Noose"—is that a wah with an envelope filter or just a wah?

THAYIL: Just a wah. But it's being used like an envelope filter, in a way. The pedal is just kind of dropped back and moved ever so slightly. We didn't make the wah sweep real fast, but made it real subtle. It's the same effect we used on "Rusty Cage," back on *Badmotorfinger*.

GW: What kind of wah was it?

THAYIL: A Colorsound—this blue thing that has built-in distortion. It's got two switches on it—one for distortion and gain and another for turning the wah on.

GW: Are any alternate tunings used on this album?

THAYIL: There's a lot of standard tuning. But three songs are in [*from low to high*] C G C G G E. On "Rhinosaur," Ben and I played in dropped-D, but Chris played in standard tuning. That's unusual for us. If one of us is in dropped-D, usually all three of us are.

GW: A history question: which was the first Seattle band to tune down?

THAYIL: I'd say the Melvins, probably. I remember a conversation I had with Buzz Osbourne. We knew that Kiss tuned their guitars down a half step. And Buzz said, "Yeah, and Sabbath went down to D." The Melvins started to use that, and we eventually started to write in dropped-D.

GW: So, it was the direct influence of the Melvins.

THAYIL: Yeah, I think so. I don't know if they would consider themselves a Seattle band, though. At the time they were living up in Montesano, which is far away. In fact, we tried to talk them into moving here: "Hell, why don't you guys just move to Seattle? You play here all the time." They said, "We don't want to live in a big city. If we're gonna live in a big city, we'd rather go somewhere like San Francisco."

GW: Tell me about writing "Never the Machine Forever." What time signature is that?

THAYIL: It's 9/8. I was jamming in the studio just for fun with Greg Gilmour, who was the drummer for Mother Love Bone, and Steve Fisk, who is the brains behind Pigeonhead and the keyboardist for Pell Mell. Greg started doing this thing that was in nine, although we didn't know it; it just seemed like some kind of tom-tom jungle music. We recorded it, listened back to it and said, "What the hell is that?" Steve and I both got lost when we tried jamming on it, because it was just, like, toms. I listened to it and started humming that riff. I went and figured it out, and from there I wrote three or four of the guitar parts. Afterwards, I showed it to the band. We arranged it, and Matt [Cameron] came up with another drum part for it. Then I spent months trying to work out the lyrics. I'm not real accustomed to writing lyrics for this band, and it's certainly more of a challenge to write them for a song that's in 9/8 as opposed to 4/4.

GW: How do you and Chris generally work out the guitar bits together on a song?

THAYIL: On the songs he writes, he plays the rhythm bits initially. Then I'll either double the rhythm bits or put little color parts down, and do a guitar solo. Chris didn't play at all on other songs, like some of the ones Ben wrote, including "An Unkind" and "Never Named." And Chris didn't play guitar on the song I wrote ["Never the Machine Forever"], or on "Applebite." On "Rhinosaur," we both played rhythm parts and I played lead. We get somewhat different sounds— he might get the brighter sound and I might get the humbucking sound. Chris generally tends to favor single-coil pickups and I lean more toward humbuckers, although I think on this record it was switched around a bit. I used a lot of Jazzmasters and Teles. I've been moving away from that Gibson humbucker kind of sound.

GW: What factors determine whose songs make it on a Soundgarden album?

THAYIL: The degree of completeness of a song. If a song doesn't have lyrics, it might hang around a bit longer. Once we have a body of material that's arranged and has lyrics—and everyone likes it—then it's all gonna make the album.

GW: I understand you had another title in mind for *Down on the Upside*.

THAYIL: Yeah, I wanted to call it *Devil—King of Children*, but some people had a problem with it.

GW: Your name is conspicuously absent from the songwriting credits on this album. Are you satisfied with your contribution?

THAYIL: No, I'm not! [*laughs*] Not at all. I used to be the primary writer. But I generally don't write lyrics that often. I have a lot of riffs and half-arranged things that might have two or three parts to them. But the arrangement usually cannot be completed without some lyrics, and so… In the case of "Never the Machine Forever," I just decided to write the lyrics myself in order to get that song completed.

GW: Is "Blow Up the Outside World" a deliberate homage to John Lennon?

THAYIL: I don't know if it's deliberate. When we first heard Chris's demo, we all kind of noticed that it was sort of Lennonish. But I don't think Chris ever said it was "deliberate."

GW: It's the line "Give you everything I've got," which is almost exactly like a line in the Beatles' "So Tired."

THAYIL: Yeah. I recognized that myself when I first heart the demo. I said, "Hey, I've heard that somewhere before."

GW: I thought it might have been a musical joke. A quotation.

THAYIL: Sometimes we might tip our hats and pay homage, or it might be a parody. But that situation… I haven't really discussed it with Chris, so I don't know.

GW: Who are your favorite guitar players from the Sixties?

THAYIL: Hendrix always comes to mind, I guess. Wayne Kramer and Fred "Sonic Smith" from the MC5, Sterling Morrison from the Velvet Underground, and Frank Zappa.

GW: Frank Zappa's influence comes out in your wah work.

THAYIL: Definitely. Yes.

GW: What about other decades?

THAYIL: Jeff Beck and Ace Frehley, from the Seventies. And from the late Seventies to early Eighties, I'd probably cite Robert Quine from the Voidoids and Tom Verlaine and that other guy from Television... I'm spacing on his name.

GW: Richard Lloyd.

THAYIL: Yeah. Then from the mid Eighties, I'd probably pick Chris Kirkwood from the Meat Puppets, Bob Mould from Hüsker Dü, D. Boone from the Minutemen, and Paul Leary from the Butthole Surfers.

GW: With those kinds of influences, how come Soundgarden has such a "metal" sound?

THAYIL: It might be just a combination of the four of us. Just our styles, I guess. It might be Chris' voice. It might be the way I play. It's all pretty natural, what we do. Put it all together and it comes out that way.

GW: Any advice for kids just starting out playing guitar?

THAYIL: Don't take lessons. Listen to your records. And watch other people play. I think the fun thing is just discovering stuff on the guitar, not having people tell you what to do. It's more fun to have it be something you explore.

GW: Guitar playing became so regimented in the late Eighties.

THAYIL: Yes, very much so. And where have those guys gone? Basically it's better on your own. Ultimately, finding a unique style and coming up with your own voice on the guitar is worth a heck of a lot more than simply being proficient.

GW: What sort of things helped you find your voice? When did your style crystallize in your own mind?

THAYIL: It probably came from just playing by myself a lot. I would sit around for hours, doodling on the guitar. And I had certain tastes in music, like a lot of the punk rock and industrial stuff from the late Seventies and early Eighties. I started writing my own stuff. And the way I wrote would usually coincide with the way I played.

GW: Good advice. Do it for yourself. Don't do it by the book.

THAYIL: Right. If you do it by the book, you'll end up sounding like the book. Many musicians who have taken lessons tell me they end up sounding like their teacher.

GW: You can tell when any musician's had lessons.

THAYIL: Yeah. There's something very proper about what they do. Although there are people who are well learned who are also very innovative.

Guitar School, August 1996

The Soft Parade

As the latest band to join MTV's hall of *Unplugged* heroes, Alice in Chains takes a detour from its dark and twisted nature to explore its sensitive side.

By Jeff Kitts

OVER ITS SIX years on the air, MTV's *Unplugged* series has become a benchmark of versatility; a pure, unadulterated forum for rock groups to play in an environment free of amps, pedals, stage effects and (for the most part) all things electronic. As demonstrated by the electrifying unplugged performances of Nirvana, the Eagles, Stone Temple Pilots and Smashing Pumpkins, playing for a few seated fans without the benefit of modern circuitry is the true test of a band's songwriting and musicianship skills. The latest rock notables to prove their soundhole savvy are Seattle's Alice in Chains.

In releasing the all-acoustic, 4-song *Sap* EP (Columbia) in 1992 (the follow-up to 1990's thunderous debut, *Facelift*), Alice in Chains guitarist Jerry Cantrell proved himself to be one of rock's more flexible fret-fliers, capable of wielding an acoustic axe as adeptly as he does his favorite electrified beast, the G&L Rampage. Cantrell's acoustic chops were further demonstrated on Alice in Chains' 1993 7-song mini-album, *Jar of Flies*, and their recent Beatles-esque smash, "Heaven Beside You."

"Once we did *Sap*," says Cantrell, "I realized that the acoustic guitar could open up a whole new world of possibilities for me as a player and songwriter. I'd say I write about 50% of our songs now on an acoustic guitar."

MTV first offered Alice in Chains an *Unplugged* special a few years ago. The band held off: a move Cantrell feels was a blessing in disguise.

"We certainly have enough material, acoustic and otherwise," says Cantrell. "But I'm glad we waited. This band is much tighter now than it used to be. Just because the opportunity is there doesn't necessarily mean that it's the right time to do something."

While the scaled-back, stripped-down, warts-and-all setting inside the Brooklyn Academy of Music, where *Unplugged* is often taped, may seem like a radical departure from the arena-sized stages the band is generally used to, Alice in Chains felt right at home and at one with a roomful of hardcore fans.

"The forum we did it in was a little different from what we're used to, but it was still just a show like any other show," says Cantrell. "We've been on a lot of different types of stages in our career, so this was actually pretty natural for us. We had a great time."

Remarkable as it may seem, the *Unplugged* session was the only concert Alice in Chains has played in over two years. But while the band remains inactive, Cantrell has kept himself plenty busy. He recently contributed a solo song called "Leave Me Alone" to the soundtrack for the film, *The Cable Guy*.

"It's certainly nice to do something else," says Cantrell. "The band can't be the only thing in your life. That's why I do what I do—it's the kind of job I always wanted."

In what is his only American interview regarding *Unplugged*, Jerry Cantrell recently spoke to *Guitar School* about the many aspects involved in taping MTV's most heralded program.

GUITAR SCHOOL: I understand you were quite sick the day of the *Unplugged* taping.
JERRY CANTRELL: Oh, I was ill that whole week. I got food poisoning from a hot dog I bought from a street vendor—bad move. I was puking right up until the gig and immediately afterward, but once

I got up there and started playing I felt fine.

GS: Playing live when you're sick must be difficult.

CANTRELL: Not really. What usually happens is that if I'm not feeling well for whatever reason, once I start playing I feel better. So when I'm sick, I look forward to getting up there and playing. It's a special thing to be able to get up there and share some tunes with the people who came to see you play.

GS: How did the offer to do *Unplugged* come about?

CANTRELL: We certainly have enough material and we could have done it a while ago, but to be honest with you, man, TV scares me. It's hard to sound good on TV, especially for a band like ours that is a little raw and rough at times. It helped me to have a friend of ours, Scottie Olsen, on stage playing guitar during the taping. It widened the sound a bit and was beneficial to the show. But I'm glad we waited to do it. Everything happens at the right time, and I think the band has never sounded better than it does now.

GS: Did you have to do any retakes during the taping?

CANTRELL: Oh yeah. We were on stage for almost three hours. It took us a few takes to get "Sludge Factory" right and we did "Got Me Wrong" four times. It's good to do different takes sometimes so you can have a choice of which version you want to put on the *Unplugged* album later. But it was cool; it extended the show, and since everyone was having such a good time, it was great. Anything to keep playing!

GS: What was the band's initial approach to doing *Unplugged*? What did you want to accomplish with it?

CANTRELL: We didn't really think about it—we just wanted to get up there and jam.

GS: How did you go about selecting which songs would work in an acoustic setting?

CANTRELL: Some songs just weeded themselves out early and some took us a while before we realized they wouldn't work. It took us a while to figure out which songs would work in that setting, and luckily, most of them did. We did material from every album except our first, *Facelift*. We almost tried "We Die Young" and "Love, Hate,

Love" from that album, but we decided not to at the last minute. That was mainly because an *Unplugged* show is only about 45 minutes when it airs, so you don't have the time to do everything.

GS: I find it interesting that you didn't do anything from *Facelift*. Except for "Man in the Box," which still gets airplay, that record almost seems like the forgotten Alice in Chains album.

CANTRELL: Hmmm...I'm not sure I agree with that. I went back and listened to it the other day and I still think it's a great album. It's real young and innocent. But it's true that a lot of people came over to us with the *Dirt* album and therefore might not be too familiar with *Facelift*.

GS: Does it mean anything special to the band to be able to do *Unplugged*? Is it anything more than just another show?

CANTRELL: I didn't look at it any other way than I've ever looked at a gig. It's a show like any other show with the band playing and people clapping and singing along and shit. I mean, that's what gets me going—that's why I do this.

GS: It's hard to imagine a song like "Sludge Factory" rendered acoustically. Did you have to do any rearranging of material to get it to work?

CANTRELL: Not really. We played everything pretty much the way it is on the records. There were a couple of jam parts in the set, but overall everything's pretty exact.

GS: How much did the band rehearse in the weeks before the taping?

CANTRELL: We messed around for a couple of weeks, but it's not like we ever really rehearse anyway. [*laughs*] Everyone always shows up at different times and we usually just end up talking and goofing around anyway. But we got in a few good rehearsals. We always kind of end up flying by the seat of our pants.

GS: *Unplugged* has an image of being a very laid back, intimate jam session between a band and a few fans, but it's still a professional television production. Is there more that goes into a taping than what's apparent on TV?

CANTRELL: Not really. It's pretty much exactly what you see. The whole thing was very laid back, very calm.

GS: Do you have to increase your awareness and attention when you do an *Unplugged* compared to a standard gig?

CANTRELL: I don't think about it that much, man. I just do it.

GS: How much had the band played together acoustically before *Unplugged*?

CANTRELL: We did a benefit show in L.A. a while ago and we played four songs from *Sap* acoustically. This was before *Jar of Flies* and all the fans were pissed because we weren't playing the heavy stuff. [*laughs*]

GS: What kind of acoustic guitars did you use on *Unplugged*?

CANTRELL: A couple of Guilds I got a hold of. They were real nice— I took them home after the taping. [*laughs*] But since I only played them once, I really don't remember much more about them other than that they sounded great.

GS: How much writing do you do on an acoustic?

CANTRELL: It really depends on whatever guitar is lying around when I get an inspiration. I've written songs on acoustic and turned them into electrics and vice versa. It really doesn't matter to me what I write on. But it's true that sometimes the guitar makes the song, like "Heaven Beside You," which was written on an acoustic.

GS: Would you say that one type of guitar suits your playing style better than the other?

CANTRELL: No, I'm pretty adaptable to any guitar, so long as the action's not too high. [*laughs*] I've been playing since I was about 17, and for the first seven or eight years, I never even touched an acoustic. But then I started fooling around with one around the time of *Sap* and I realized that I could do different things on an acoustic.

GS: There's an interesting balance to Alice in Chains' music, a combination of dark, twisted, highly electrified sections and softer, prettier, acoustic stuff.

CANTRELL: I'm thankful for that fact. It keeps our music interesting and gives us a lot of room to do different things. Led Zeppelin was definitely a big influence in that area; Page could go from one end of the spectrum to the other, often in the same song.

GS: What other bands did you listen to while you were growing up that handled acoustic guitars creatively?

CANTRELL: Pink Floyd, definitely. I was a big Floyd fan. Thin Lizzy, Scorpions, Sabbath, Randy Rhoads. Even Metallica was awesome at the dark/light thing.

GS: Oddly, though, aside from "Heaven Beside You" and "Over Now," there seems to be a lack of acoustic guitars on *Alice in Chains*.

CANTRELL: I disagree with you. There's a lot of acoustic stuff on this album, a lot of flavoring in different places.

GS: It still seems as if you save a lot of your *wholly* acoustic songs for EPs like *Sap* and *Jar of Flies*.

CANTRELL: *Sap* and *Jar of Flies* were just fun projects that we did; we were just fucking around and never intended for them to be big records or anything. But it's true that our records have always been real heavy. That's not a conscious decision on our part; we don't sit around and think about what kind of songs we want on an album—they just end up that way.

GS: Have you ever played acoustic guitars on stage?

CANTRELL: No, except that benefit in L.A.

GS: Do you think the *Unplugged* experience will entice you to play some acoustic songs when you play live again?

CANTRELL: Probably. It makes sense, now that we've done it. But the truth is that the great thing about playing live is being able to go wild, and you really can't do that with an acoustic guitar. I think the whole band was a bit frustrated during *Unplugged* because it was such a controlled environment and we weren't able to just plug in and rip out. [*laughs*]

GS: How did the offer to do a solo track ("Leave Me Alone") on the *Cable Guy* soundtrack come about?

CANTRELL: That was really fun. I met with the director, Ben Stiller, at a video shoot in Los Angeles, and he asked me if I wanted to do something. I already had some material I had worked on prior to doing the *Alice in Chains* record, and when Ben heard it he said, 'That's great!' After I went back and listened to it, I realized that the lyrics kind of fit the vibe of the movie, which I hadn't planned on when I wrote them. The whole thing was just a good opportunity for me to do something else. We're not on tour right now, so why not?

GS: Who's the backing band on the track?

CANTRELL: It's just me and Sean [*Kinney, Alice in Chains' drummer*]. I play guitar and bass and I sing.

GS: This is the first time you've done something by yourself, outside of the band. Is it weird to have solo billing?

CANTRELL: Yeah, it is weird. But that's okay because my heart has always been in Alice in Chains, and that's what's most important.

GS: How did the rest of Alice in Chains react when they found out it was a Cantrell solo track?

CANTRELL: I don't know. I didn't seem to get too much flak over it. [*laughs*] There's a certain sense of loyalty in this band because we've been together for a long time. We're all talented and there are other things out there, so we don't stop each other from trying other things. The band can't be the only thing you do.

GS: Does the band have plans for the rest of the summer?

CANTRELL: I don't know—I really can't say right now. We'd like to get out there and maybe do some touring…yeah, that would be nice.

DAVE GROHL of FOO FIGHTERS

Guitar World, August 1997

Absolutely Foobulous!

The Foo Fighters' Dave Grohl and Pat Smear talk rock fashion, reminisce about Nirvana and praise their new old-fashioned group effort, *The Colour and the Shape*.

By Alan di Perna

N THE DANK half-light of a North Hollywood rehearsal room, Pat Smear strokes his chin meditatively as he selects a guitar for the night's work ahead. Hmm, should he go with his opulent Gretsch White Falcon or his el cheapo Asian SG copy? Decisions, decisions. Only a mind as unconventional as Smear's could hold the two instruments in equal esteem. Towering over his guitar rack in a pair of red plaid trousers that accentuate his tall, slim frame, Smear opts to go Gretsch this time.

A few paces away, Taylor Hawkins sits on the floor in front of his drum kit, shirtless and pale-skinned, like some schoolboy gone savage in a scene from *Lord of the Flies*. The drummer, who'd been regaling his bandmates with an a cappella medley of tacky Eighties pop hits, pauses to belch resonantly. Wonder how his former bandleader, Alanis Morissette, would've enjoyed that? But it takes more than a rude noise to disrupt the guy world of the Foo Fighters. Over in a corner, Nate Mendel fiddles with his bass rig, with the serene, astute air of a class nerd with his pet science project.

Suddenly, Dave Grohl bursts through the door. Just off the plane from Japan, the chief Foo is still running on crazy, jet-lagged energy. Tall, lanky, and sporting a full goatee these days, he bounds across the room and straps on a tobacco sunburst Les Paul. In an instant, the three other musicians are all focused and charged up, like their leader. They launch into "Everlong," a guitar-fueled, quintessential alt-rock Nineties tune from the new Foo Fighters album, *The Colour and the Shape* (Capitol). Grohl obligingly pauses to show me the chords: a series of barre shapes against an open sixth string tuned down to D.

"I have no idea what these chords are called," he declares with punky aplomb.

He sure can play 'em, though. A multi-faceted talent, Grohl did the drumming that propelled Nirvana to Nineties rock supremacy. But he started out on guitar. "Actually, my first instrument was trombone, when I was seven or eight years old," says Grohl, "but I started playing guitar when I was 10." Not long after, he was playing in the mid-Eighties hardcore punk scene in the Washington, D.C., area, where he grew up. A personnel shift in his very first band, Freak Baby, led him to lay down his guitar and get behind a drum kit. He pummeled the skins for a variety of D.C. bands—Mission Impossible, Dain Bramage and Scream—before being asked out to Seattle to join Kurt Cobain and Krist Novoselic just in time to record Nirvana's landmark *Nevermind*.

But Grohl always kept his guitar handy, and eventually began writing songs on it. "When Nirvana was on tour, I'd bring a guitar with me," he says, "so in hotel rooms, late at night, I'd have something to do. Since Kurt was left-handed, I learned how to play a left-handed guitar right-handed. But I just started bringing my own out with me. And at home there was always a guitar next to the couch, or on the bed, or in front of the TV. I love playing the drums, but you can't really sit down at home with a snack and play the drums. So I've never been without a guitar. Eventually, I was living with a person who had an 8-track in the basement. And these songs just started coming out."

Those songs eventually formed the basis for the first Foo Fighters album. Recovering from his initial shock and grief at the death of Kurt Cobain and the end of Nirvana, Grohl went in the studio and recorded *Foo Fighters* entirely on his own (save for one guest guitar track by Greg Dulli of the Afghan Whigs). But somewhere between the tracking and the mixing of the record, the Foo Fighters went from being an imaginary band to a real one. Grohl didn't have to look far for a co guitarist. Pat Smear had played with Nirvana during the band's final phase. A punk rock originator, he'd played guitar with the legendary Germs, which made him a rock and roll hero to both Cobain and Grohl.

Nate Mendel and drummer William Goldsmith—who had played with Sunny Day Real Estate and whom Grohl knew from around the Seattle scene—became the Foo Fighters' rhythm section. Goldsmith dropped out of the band during sessions for *The Colour and the Shape*, leaving Grohl to finish up the drums on the record. Shortly after the disc was completed, Morrisette alumnus Taylor Hawkins was recruited as the Foo Fighters' new drummer.

When Grohl is hanging around with the other Foos, he's very much one of the guys. But when they man their instruments and start to play, a subtle transformation occurs: Grohl clearly emerges as the leader. Not that he becomes bossy or domineering. He's just quietly in command. The vision is his; after all, he writes the songs. But for all that, *The Colour and the Shape* was a group effort, with band members all contributing to the arrangements. As a result, says Grohl, it's a better disc than the first Foo Fighters album. *The Colour and the Shape* certainly shows signs of natural and healthy growth. There are bits that rock harder than its predecessor, and mellower moments of acoustic balladry. But most of all, there's plenty of that pop-smart overdrive that made the first album such a monster success.

"I just have so much faith in those guys," says Grohl of his bandmates. "If I come in with the most ridiculous three-chord, verse/chorus/verse idea, I know they can make it into something great.

Without them, this album would have sounded thinner and less interesting. That's why I'm so proud of it. Everybody threw in their two cents and it came out as this big sound."

As personalities, Grohl and Smear are pretty dissimilar. Smear's a first-generation punk and Grohl is quintessentially second-generation, but they seem to navigate that vast youth-cult chasm with easy grace. Smear is L.A. to the max. He's into that flashy, slightly ironic embrace of trash culture that L.A. living seems to inspire, and has that soft, uniquely Angeleno way of speaking that is equal parts Valley Girl and Hollywood hipster. Grohl, for his part, exudes the straightedge, "I'm not a rock star" sincerity of the D.C. hardcore scene. He seems like the kind of person who busses his own tray at fast food restaurants. But day-and-night opposites always make the best teams. Grohl and Smear are no exception, whether they're playing guitars or dressing up for a photo shoot.

GUITAR WORLD: Some of the editors at *Guitar World* were really taken with the fact that, at the photo shoot for this story, you guys were wearing a lot of designer stuff.
DAVE GROHL: We had a stylist. That's where I got these pants I'm wearing.
GW: For the shoot, both of you guys were in Gucci, Prada…
PAT SMEAR: Yeah, what's up with that anyways?
GW: What is up with that?
SMEAR: I just love to dress up. It could be designer clothes or a clown suit, it doesn't matter. And yes, I have gone on stage in a clown suit—when I was in 45 Grave. They were into all this scary, ghoul, Goth makeup. You know, we had the devil on guitar and a skeleton on drums. And I was like, "Okay, I'm gonna dress up like a clown." It was actually just as scary as everyone else in the band. So I've always been into dressing up.
GROHL: Pat has always been famous for his fashion sense. But I can't imagine walking on stage in anything but jeans and a T-shirt. The last thing I want to do is go on stage in a Dolce and Gabana suit and ruin it by jumping around and sweating it up. I'll stick with a T-shirt,

thank you very much.

GW: People tend to associate the Seattle aesthetic more with dressing down.

SMEAR: Yeah, I was never into the dressing down thing. There's a difference between being a slob and dressing down. I've always been a slob. But you can be a slob with style. But when there's a dressing down scene—where dressing down is your uniform—then it's just as dumb as hairspray metal. There are some people I actually feel bad for, like Mike Watt. At this point, he can't wear anything but jeans and Converse and Pendleton. He can't. He's just pigeonholed himself into that too much. Same thing with Eddie Vedder, who cannot go out in a Gucci suit without getting laughed at now. As far as I'm concerned, those people blew it. I'm so lucky; I can wear anything I want and it's like, "Oh well, that's Pat."

GW: Punk was always about dressing up—at first, anyway.

SMEAR: Punk was dressing up. We had barriers and certain limits, but it was still about dressing up. Then, in the Eighties punk scene they were all dressing like that, and I thought, "Well, now you're just copying. Why bother? Like wow, you look just like a band you saw in a photo from 1978." Don't get me wrong, I love seeing kids in mohawks, but it just doesn't have the same impact as it did back in the day when people would scream out their car window at you and want to kick your ass if you had a mohawk. I mean there's secretaries with blue hair these days. So it's not really any big deal.

GW: What's your take on the current state of rock, post-grunge, late Nineties?

GROHL: I like the new Supergrass record. I like the Cardigans. I like Oasis—their music anyway. I don't know. I like all different kinds of music. I love the Prodigy, Bjork...as long as there's a song in there somewhere, it's cool. But I don't know. There's also a lot of crap. But what are you gonna do, you know?

GW: There's no single reigning style right now, which allows all kinds of sounds to come through.

GROHL: Yeah, it's kinda nice. Hopefully, eventually, the whole brooding, Fender Jaguar grunge style will go away. It isn't gone yet. It will be soon, though. And it'll be time for some good old Les Paul, southern rock. [laughs]

GW: The Foo Fighters have always maintained a balance of pop melodicism and harder, "grunge" elements. Is that just a natural combination of things for you, or a very carefully worked out mixture?

GROHL: We all love music, whether it's the Beatles or Queen or punk rock. I think the lure of punk rock was the energy and immediacy; the need to thrash stuff around. But at the same time, we're all suckers for a beautiful melody, you know? So it is just natural. I loved the Beatles when I was a kid, but I loved the Bad Brains too. And there were a lot of bands in the early to mid Eighties that were a perfect blend of those things. Hüsker Dü had a searing guitar sound and breakneck speeds, but they'd do that as they were covering the Byrds' "Eight Miles High." It was just beautiful and powerful. I think that's probably where it all comes from. It's not necessarily blueprinted or calculated. It's just the way we like to play.

SMEAR: Punk was the first music I played in a band. But it wasn't the first music I was into. I was into Queen, Bowie and Alice Cooper—that Seventies pop rock glam kind of thing.

GW: Dave, do you feel that Kurt Cobain was a big influence on you as a songwriter?

GROHL: Kurt was definitely a big influence and inspiration. When I first moved up to Washington state, I lived with Kurt in this tiny apartment. For the longest time, we didn't have a television. We didn't have anything to do. So we'd spend these gray Olympia, Washington, afternoons just playing guitars and messing around with a 4-track, or working on harmonies. Through Kurt, I saw the beauty of minimalism and the importance of music that's stripped down. That's more powerful, because it's just so...almost desperate, you know? So in that way, yeah, Kurt was a great influence.

GW: A sense of stark contrasts is one common element between Nirvana and the Foo Fighters. Sweet verses that give way to abrasive choruses, the whole loud/soft dynamic that set the blueprint for Nineties alternative rock—where did all that come from?

GROHL: From Kurt, Krist and I liking the Knack, Bay City Rollers,

Beatles and Abba just as much as we liked Flipper and Black Flag, I suppose. The dynamics thing specifically came out of this four-month period before *Nevermind* was recorded, where we were rehearsing maybe five days a week for three or four hours a day, just writing songs and jams and stuff like that. And we just started experimenting with these really extreme dynamics. It's not like we were the first band to do it. You listen to any Pixies record and it's all over there. Or even Black Sabbath's "War Pigs"—it's there: the power of the dynamic. We just sort of abused it with pop songs and got sick with it—silly with it. It was fun. feeling good in some mellow verse and then smashing your way into some big, huge, distorted chorus. I suppose it's a cheap way to make the chorus seem a lot bigger than it really is.

GW: You joined Nirvana kind of "in progress," Dave. Kurt and Krist started it.

GROHL: Yeah, I was their seventh drummer.

GW: So did you really feel fully a part of where they were coming from?

GROHL: Where they were coming from, yeah. But I always felt kind of expendable. When you're the seventh drummer, it would be pretty big-headed of you to imagine yourself being the *final* drummer.

GW: Did that sense remain throughout?

GROHL: That feeling that I was the umpteenth millionth drummer? Yeah. I mean, I felt comfortable with it. I didn't feel unwanted. I felt like I was doing my duty and I was doing it okay. But yeah, it was always sort of in the back of my mind. It would be hard for it not to be.

GW: Was that a factor in your always writing songs on your own—why you had a musical life and identity apart from Nirvana?

GROHL: Not really. When you're in a band with somebody like Kurt, who was an amazing songwriter, you do anything you can to keep from polluting the songwriting process. I thought, "I don't want to be the person responsible for ruining these songs." There's a famous old joke: What was the last thing the drummer said before they kicked him out of the band? "Hey guys, I got a new song I just wrote." Why fix it, if it ain't busted? I was in awe of what was happening. I was in awe of Kurt's songs. And intimidated. I felt it was best that I keep my songs to myself.

GW: You didn't play them for anyone?

GROHL: Yeah. I was always really freaked out about singing and my voice. I still am, kind of. But every once in a while I'd play a tape for a friend and try to have them guess who it was. They'd be like, "Is this the new Sloan record? Who is this?" "No, it's me." There are probably seven or eight people in the world that heard any of this stuff before the album came out. It was really just because I was embarrassed and shy. When you play big loud drums in a rock band five days a week, hitting them as hard as you can, when it comes to something as delicate as an acoustic melody, it's a little scary. You're really putting yourself on the line.

SMEAR: When Nirvana was rehearsing, before we went out on tour, there was a day when Dave came in and played me a tape of the stuff he was working on at home. Some of those things were probably the songs I've played thousands of times for the past two years with the Foo Fighters.

GW: Dave recorded the first Foo Fighters album all on his own. When did Pat, Nate and William get involved?

SMEAR: The first activity we ever did as a band was mixing the first album. We didn't play on it, but the whole band sat together in some studio in Northern California and mixed it. It was kind of weird. Even though we didn't play on it, we felt like it was our record, because we were all having our input and our say in the mix.

GW: For the new album, *The Colour and the Shape*, was there more songwriting involvement on the band's part?

SMEAR: Well, Dave still wrote all the songs. But we'd all come in and work on them—change them and see what needed to be done with them.

GROHL: It took more time that way, but ultimately it was far more rewarding. Because when I record something by myself, I can hear what the final version will sound like before I start. It's that predictable, which makes the end result kind of one-dimensional and not as powerful.

GW: Where did you record the new album?

SMEAR: We recorded in Woodinville, which is half an hour out of Seattle, at a studio in a converted barn. There was a house there, and we all lived together and recorded an album. Then we basically scrapped it and came down to L.A. and recorded another album. It wasn't our intention to do it that way. But since I live in L.A., I left Woodinville early while the other guys finished up their overdubs. We figured we'd mix in L.A. and, before mixing began, just book a couple of weeks in a studio and finish all my guitar parts and vocals. But we ended up re-recording the whole thing, pretty much.

GW: Where did you record in L.A.?

SMEAR: Grand Master Studios, a cool little divey studio on Cahuenga, near Sunset.

GROHL: Grand Master was amazing. It used to be a silent movie theater. And they had this huge garage out back where we did a lot of the drums and got the most amazing room sound.

GW: So what happened with William?

GROHL: He wasn't into the recording method we used. He's a great drummer, but when we went into the studio it just didn't pan out. I think we may have gone into the studio too soon. Because from the last show that we had in Europe, in August, to the beginning of rehearsals, in the middle of September, we had eight or nine songs that we hadn't even tapped into yet. And then we got into the studio, where everything's gotta be right on the mark, and it just wasn't really his thing, you know. So we came back to L.A. and tried to do things differently. I played drums on stuff, and we started to rearrange the songs and basically re-recorded almost everything.

Also, after a year-and-a-half of touring, I think William just wasn't into it anymore. He wanted to play with other people. We understood that. There wasn't too much drama to it. We were building up to doing this recording, got real excited about it, and then it didn't happen right off the bat. We worked at it and tried a lot of different things; by the end, it was exhausting.

GW: Which songs were recorded for the first time in L.A.?

SMEAR: "Everlong." We also added "Walking After You," which is one the band didn't play on. Dave did that as a demo in D.C. when he was home for Christmas. He liked it that way.

GW: Did anything from the Woodinville sessions make it onto the album?

SMEAR: "Doll" did. Also "The Colour and the Shape" [*a non-album B side*]. But "Monkey Wrench," "Hey, Johnny Park!," "My Hero," "February Stars" and "New Way Home" we re-did from scratch in L.A. I think "My Poor Brain" and "Up in Arms" ended up being a combination of tracks from Woodinville and L.A.

GW: Would you two say your approach to guitar playing is similar?

SMEAR: It seems like our intentions are a lot different when we play, but in the end it comes out pretty much the same. The only way you'd be able to know isn't by our songs but when we're just fucking around in the studio. Dave can actually pull off the rock leads and stuff like that.

GROHL: Pat's nuts. You think of Pat as being the punkest of the punk, but he taught me how to play "Blackbird." [*laughs*] It's really hard. He's a great guitar player.

GW: So, when you're coming up with guitar arrangements you don't really see it as a lead/rhythm thing?

SMEAR: I'm all about rhythm. I'm anti-lead. I've been in bands before where I had to pay lead. I've had enough of that. Rhythm guitar players get no respect.

GROHL: I think there's maybe only one lead on the record. I don't really know how to do leads. I think if a song doesn't need a solo, then why put one in? I've got nothing to show off, that's for sure.

GW: Was it you who played the leads on "Walking After You"?

GROHL: Yeah, that was me.

GW: That's good stuff.

GROHL: Well, see, I wouldn't even consider that a lead. But something like "Monkey Wrench" [*sings descending guitar figure*], I'll do that. But to me that's more part of the song than a "lead." I don't really know what I'm doing. I just try and do what sounds right.

GROHL: Did you tune down or use any alternate tunings on this record?

SMEAR: "Monkey Wrench," "Hey, Johnny Park!" "February Stars" and "Everlong" are in dropped D. On "See You," I tuned the high E string on my guitar up to G. I used my Burns baritone guitar on a few songs, and I tuned that up to B. Otherwise, it just sounded like a bass. You couldn't play chords. So I just tuned it so high it felt like the strings were going to snap, which was where the E string was up to B and so on down the line.

GW: A fifth higher!

SMEAR: Yeah. And then I put a capo on it, and after doing all that I intonated it for that tuning with that capo. That made it sound great. I used it on "My Hero" and "Dear Lover" [*another non-album B-side*] and, I think, something else, but I don't remember what. It was one of the last things I did on the record, and it sounded so good I just wanted to go back and redo everything with it.

GW: You had years and years to write the first album, Dave. This time, you had to produce a whole second album reasonably quickly. Was that difficult?

GROHL: Not really, 'cause I don't actually do anything but sit around and play music. We went in originally with 25 songs, and 13 of those made it onto the record. We had a lot of material to choose from. Being on tour for a year-and-a-half, we had a lot of time to fool around with new material during soundchecks.

GW: When do you write the lyrics?

GROHL: Usually the last minute. On this album we'd written all the music before I started thinking, "Oh God, I gotta start writing words, 'cause there's gonna be a lyric sheet on this record." I'm really intimidated by lyrics. My father was a writer; my mother was an English teacher. So whenever I write lyrics, I always expect them to come back with a grade on top of the page. With the first record, those lyrics were really put under a microscope—people were reading way too much into them. They were some of the most ridiculous, nonsensical lyrics I ever heard in my life, and people were desperately fishing around for all kinds of meanings in them. It was annoying, you know? So I thought, "Okay, this time I gotta spell it out for them in black and white." I wanted things to be understandable.

GW: Is "My Hero" about anyone in particular?

GROHL: It's about a bunch of people. When I was young, I didn't have sports heroes. I had "guitar heroes," but they didn't really mean that much for me. So my heroes were just people in my life that I had a lot of respect for. They were people that I know that just seemed like ordinary people. What, do kids look up to Dennis Rodman as a hero? What for—wanting to be six- or 10-feet tall so you can put a basketball in a hoop? That's just not my kind of hero.

GW: That's the song people are going to think is about Kurt Cobain.

GROHL: I'm sure. People have already said that: " 'My Hero' is obviously about Kurt." And, in a way, it is. But there's nothing wrong with that.

GW: But it's not only about him? Is that what you're saying?

GROHL: Yeah. Basically, it's about the power of the ordinary person.

GW: Vocally, was Kurt an influence on you?

GROHL: I don't know. He had such a unique voice. He was such a great singer. I don't know if I could ever pull that off. I don't really think I have too many vocal influences. Obviously Charles [*Black Francis, a.k.a. Frank Black*] from the Pixies, and Mark Lanegan, the singer from the Screaming Trees, although I don't hear any of his stylings in my vocals.

GW: You get off a nice third-verse scream in "Monkey Wrench."

GROHL: Yeah, well a lot of my favorite vocalists are in hardcore bands. There's a hardcore band from Texas called Crucifix. The fuckin' singer in that band has a blood-curdling voice. And I always liked Henry Rollins, and Keith Morris from the Circle Jerks. I loved his voice, man. 'Cause he had this real Californian accent. So a lot of my vocal heroes are hardcore singers. I never considered myself a singer. I can scream really good. But when it comes to singing, I don't know, man.

GW: In the recording studio, is it hard to get into that state of really being able to scream your head off?

GROHL: No. That's the easy part. The hard part is really having to *sing*. When you write a song that deserves a beautiful vocal line because the melody is already there, and the texture, and you have to put the cherry on top with the vocals—that's when it gets scary. The song sounds great, but you haven't put vocals on yet. Then after you do, you think, "Great, I just ruined the song." That's where the pressure comes in.

GW: How did you find your new drummer, Taylor Hawkins?

GROHL: We did some shows in Europe with the Alanis Morissette band and met him then. He's an amazing drummer and a hilarious guy. We hit it off immediately. After William left, I called Taylor to ask him if he knew of any drummer who would want to "fill the stool." [*laughs*] And he offered his services. I thought, "Shit!" 'Cause you don't get much better than Taylor; you really don't. He's the best drummer I've ever known. He can do anything—play like John Bonham, play like Stewart Copeland, play jazz. He plays piano and guitar; he's got a beautiful voice; he's just amazing.

GW: Do drummers tend to be intimidated by working in a band with you?

GROHL: Yeah, for whatever reason I don't know. I'm so incredibly overrated as a drummer. I'm just a minimalist drummer. I am. I swear. I'm not there to do anything but propel the song.

GW: But you do it in a way that no one else does.

GROHL: I dunno. Since Taylor's in the band, I don't even get behind the drum set 'cause he makes me feel like a fool. I watch him do all this crazy stuff, then I sit down and do an AC/DC beat! He's so far out of my league, it isn't funny.

GW: Do you tend to be very specific about drum arrangements?

GROHL: Not really. If there needs to be an accent or something in a song, I won't say, "Okay, here's what you do: kick, snare, ride, and then the two floor toms." I just say, "Bring this part up a little bit." I mean, Taylor already knows. Being a guitar player who's also a drummer, I understand the relationship between the two instruments. And Taylor is a drummer who's also a guitar player, so he understands it too. So there's not much I really need to explain to him. People who understand song structures and riffs don't have much trouble feeling their way through a song. They can just sense when things need to come down, when things need to repeat, and when there needs to be an accent.

GW: There's such a thing as rhythmic intelligence.

GROHL: Yeah, look at someone like J Mascis, who is an amazing drummer and a wailing guitar player too. He understands the relationship between the two. Look at [*the artist formerly known as*] Prince—same thing.

GW: All those guys understand the rhythmic potential of the guitar.

GROHL: I wonder if James Hetfield knows how to play the drums. Because, basically, he's taking care of the percussion and the melody of Metallica's songs with his guitar.

GW: That chunking.

GROHL: Yeah. And it's great. There's the relationship right there.

KRIST NOVASELIC

Guitar World, August 1997

For Krist's Sake

Onetime Nirvana bassist Krist Novoselic resurrects his musical self with the help of a new power trio, a 12-string guitar and an exciting, eclectic debut.

By Tom Gogola

IMAGINE IF, AT the frenzied height of Nirvana's celebrity in 1992, a fortune teller had peered into her crystal ball and declared to bassist Krist Novoselic: "Five years hence, you will put out an album that features you on 12-string electric guitar. It will also include a Herb Alpert trumpet solo, a 'power lounge' track and a Venezuelan folk-blues, sung in Spanish by a green-haired female whose voice sounds, at times, like Burton Cummings from the Guess Who."

No doubt Novoselic, party animal that he was in '92, would have looked that fortune teller in the eye and said, "Say, let me have what you're drinking."

But here it is, five years down the road, and every one of those seemingly egregious predictions has come true. Novoselic's new band, Sweet 75, featuring the Venezuelan bassist/singer Yva Las Vegas and former Ministry drummer Bill Rieflin, finds the onetime Nirvana bassist playing most of the guitars. On the three tracks which spotlight Las Vegas' exemplary chops, Novoselic mans his former spot in the bass hole.

If the eclectic nature of Sweet 75's debut on Geffen seems a jarring stylistic lurch into frankly and unapologetically uncommercial territory, Novoselic insists it's not a deliberate one. And besides, *anything* Novoselic does now would, more than likely, come up short against the massive commercial success of all things Nirvana.

In the three years since Novoselic's best friend and bandmate, Kurt Cobain, took his own life, Novoselic has kept a relatively low profile—especially when compared to the enthusiasm with which former Nirvana drummer Dave Grohl's band, Foo Fighters, leaped into the void. Shattered by Cobain's death, Novoselic hung up his bass, quit drinking, bought a farm outside Seattle and helped put out the Nirvana live album last year. He also set to work on getting his national lobbying organization, the Joint Artists and Musicians Political Action Coalition (JAMPAC), off the ground. JAMPAC, says Novoselic, exists to fight against censorship, cabaret laws and other issues of interest to musicians and young persons.

Seated high up in a midtown Manhattan skyscraper, in the cavernous bowels of the Geffen Empire of fine musical products, Novoselic sits with his feet sprawled atop a long conference table. Yva Las Vegas' feet join his, nearly touching at the center of the table. Novoselic, ever on the lookout for the best interests of his bandmate, at one point reaches across and dislodges a stone caught in the tread of her chunky black boots. There's a sweet, sibling-like quality to their relationship.

"I'm the older, more experienced woman in the band," says the diva, who at 33 is one year older than Novoselic.

"She's like my older sister," he concurs.

GUITAR WORLD: You waited several years between the end of Nirvana and the release of the Sweet 75 debut. Did you go into the studio thinking, "I'm going to make an antidote to all things grunge?"
KRIST NOVOSELIC: No. We went into the studio, worked on the music, listened to the songs, and everything we did, we did for the song. And it all just came together.
YVA LAS VEGAS: We didn't know what it was going to sound like. There were two different tastes here, two different styles, two different people coming together to make music. And it's going to

sound different from what he did or what I did before. It's a matter of chemistry.

NOVOSELIC: That's a good way of putting it—the chemistry and the way everybody had to approach their respective instrument in a new way. We were all in a situation where we weren't doing things conventionally—I was playing guitar, Yva was playing bass and Bill was doing more expressive, free-form drumming than he had done in Ministry.

GW: The label wanted to wait a bit before releasing the finished album, but were there any other reasons—personal reasons?

NOVOSELIC: No. We were really hot to trot. But the label, God bless 'em, said "Take your time, keep developing." We were getting kind of frustrated, but in hindsight, it was the right thing. We said, "We want to open for this pop band because they're selling records." And they said, "Oh, no, no, no, you've got to open for Dinosaur Jr."

GW: You could just as easily be opening for the Gypsy Kings with this album.

NOVOSELIC: Think so?! Wow. I'd love that.

GW: Geffen, I've heard, didn't want your album and the Foo Fighters record coming out at the same time, to avoid that inevitable "former Nirvana" angle.

NOVOSELIC: I'm really afraid of getting trapped in those kinds of perspectives, know what I mean?

GW: No.

NOVOSELIC: In developing the band, there were mines and traps all around us. We had different perspectives confronting us at every turn: "If we do it this way, people will think that; if we do it the other way, they'll think this."

GW: What are some of the mines?

NOVOSELIC: What are some of the mines? Well, anything involved with Nirvana, or the media, the whole Nirvana-media circus, or what Nirvana has become, compared to what it actually was. If we'd taken those perspectives and applied them to the music we were making, it would have been a disaster. We would have lost a limb, or it would have been lethal. Just like a mine. Mines are terrible.

GW: You don't seem to have the need, or the desire even, to "say something" about Nirvana on this album. Why is that?

NOVOSELIC: Why? Well, I'm still dealing with a lot of that stuff, and I don't know what I want to say about it. There's lots to say, there's nothing to say. There's so much being said, I'm tired of it.

GW: Do you see what you're doing now in any way as being part of some kind of healing process?

NOVOSELIC: Oh, yeah. Part of it is just to help me move on. I'm really excited to be playing again. I didn't plan on this. I quit drinking in November of 1994, and that was really a new experience for me. Not being drunk all the time, I had all this energy. I was doing the band, I was doing politics, a radio show, all this stuff. The bottom line is that music is the priority again, and I'm happy with that and happy to have the opportunity. I'm very lucky. I like to call this a band, because if I wasn't happy with it, it would be a project.

GW: Have you noticed anyone trying to pigeonhole Sweet 75 in that way, to not take it seriously because it's so unlike what you've done before?

NOVOSELIC: I don't think so, because we don't have a lot of other perspectives on this band right now. We've been very low key, haven't done much press or much playing out.

LAS VEGAS: We have had the "It's Krist Novoselic's band" thing. It sucks, but that's going to happen.

NOVOSELIC: When we opened for Sky Cries Mary and Dinosaur, people came out just for the Nirvana factor, which created kind of a circus. That's why I'm looking forward to releasing this record, so the band can be judged on its own merits. And that whole cult of celebrity thing… I was talking before about how Nirvana should apply for tax-free status as a religion, because of how the fans have deified Kurt. Maybe that's one way to get something positive out of all of this. I'm thinking about it.

GW: Have you ever thought about what Cobain might have thought of your new band?

NOVOSELIC: Well, I had a dream once with Kurt in it, and I was so glad to see him. I said, "Oh, you've got to meet Yva, you'd love her."

And I started telling him, "Check out my new band." I try not to think, "what would he think," because I don't think it's appropriate.

GW: Can you hear people saying, "The last thing I thought I'd find on Krist Novoselic's first album after Nirvana is songs sung in Spanish, and [*A&M Records president and former Tijuana Brass trumpeter*] Herb Alpert."

NOVOSELIC: In a lot of ways Nirvana was just a straightforward, heavy rock band. The songs were different, and there were a lot of dynamics on the records. But Nirvana always did try to have a mixed bag of songs, and that's the same in Sweet 75. Each song has its own personality. I think a lot of it is due to us working on this record with Paul [Fox]. He's not really a heavy rock producer guy, like Butch Vig, Andy Wallace, Steve Albini—the guys Nirvana recorded with. He's more of a low-key, mainstream guy. He's definitely strong on the vocals, and he's a keyboard player, so we added keys to a lot of the tracks. That was all added for color—that was Paul's word: "Let's add a little color here." That's how the horn section idea for "La Vida" happened. We thought, "Well, let's just have fun and try it out. Herb Alpert…"

GW: Yes, Herb Alpert! How did he wind up on your album?

LAS VEGAS: It started with a passing comment. When it came up that we'd like to get him, it was a joke: "Yeah, right."

NOVOSELIC: Never happen.

LAS VEGAS: And then it turned out that the engineer knew him really well and knew Herb's manager…

NOVOSELIC: …Eddie Thacker. And Herb's label [*A&M*] is affiliated with Geffen. That's one of the bonuses of having a five-year relationship with Geffen: you can make the call to Herb Alpert. Herb heard the song, liked it, and laid a solo down. It's a great, beautiful solo.

GW: Were you there when he recorded it?

NOVOSELIC: No, no. We never even met him. I wanted to meet him so we could say he's a great guy, a beautiful man. We wanted to. We're going to. He took the time out to do it at his home studio, and I'm sure he's a very busy man. We really appreciated it.

LAS VEGAS: That was a real big compliment.

NOVOSELIC: Plus my mom was very excited. [*laughs*]

GW: Is that one of the things that motivates you in this band, Krist? To have a lot of style shifting and work with the challenges it presents?

NOVOSELIC: It does. It is a great challenge to keep things interesting, especially in the context of a guitar, bass, drums and vocals.

GW: Do you ever joke, or argue, about who the better guitar player in the band is?

LAS VEGAS & NOVOSELIC: No! No way!

GW: Yva, did you write the song "Cantos de Pilon"?

LAS VEGAS: No, no. That's a traditional work song. Nobody even knows who the author is—it's one of those kinds of songs.

NOVOSELIC: It's a Venezuelan blues.

LAS VEGAS: I've loved it since I was five years old. It's like a blues, because people who sing it make new lyrics up. In this song, the workers are grinding corn and they are all insulting each other a bit while they work, and talking about life and love and work, and things like that. It's pretty.

GW: What was the instrumentation on this song, Krist?

NOVOSELIC: Well, I played accordion on it, and Bill played the piano and Peter Buck played the mandolin. And that song was done totally live. We sat down and recorded three or four takes and took the best one. There's that one drum in there, and that was Peter's idea. He is just so much fun to play with.

LAS VEGAS: It came together so easily.

GW: And the song "Nothing," which follows it, is a massive, minorkey dirge-rocker. Are those arpeggios and the chord progression at the bridge all your playing, Krist?

NOVOSELIC: Yeah. That's more unconventional stuff. I just play the one pair of strings, then into the arpeggios. That's kind of a weird song, and I really like the lyrics to it.

GW: What are they about?

LAS VEGAS: Oh, they're sad. It's about my mom dying.

GW: That song sounded to me like circa-1985 prototype college radio rock, like the early stuff from Urge Overkill. No overdrive, everything out front. Kind of ground zero indie rock.

NOVOSELIC: Wow. *Essential.*

LAS VEGAS: The equipment we use is part of that. Krist doesn't use a wall of Marshalls, he's got two amps and he doesn't use tons of pedals, just a distortion pedal.

NOVOSELIC: The amps are an Orange Combo—an old one, and I'm not going to use that one anymore, it's more of a collector piece—and a reissue Vox AC 30. I'm going to switch to a HiWatt stack. We run our stuff this way: On Yva's side of the stage, there's the AC 30 and an Ampeg bass amp cab, 8 x 10; on my side, there's another bass cab and the Orange, so that when we switch we can still hear everything.

I don't know if that explains everything. I remember playing guitar in 1985 with Buzz from the Melvins, and Kurt, and there was definitely what you called that Eighties approach to guitar; it was kind of freaked-out sounding. I guess I was starting all over again with Sweet 75 and went back to that period.

GW: Are you excited about going back out on the road?

NOVOSELIC: I guess I am. I'm kind of weary of it, just because of reading a lot of rock magazines and looking at TV and not being interested in it, and here I am doing it: promoting this record, touring. I've got to put the game face on.

GW: It's pretty unusual for somebody to play the 12-string for more than one or two jangly tracks on an album. Why did you use it for the whole album?

LAS VEGAS: Because he had one! [*laughs*]

NOVOSELIC: When Yva and I first got together, we wrote songs on a 12-string I had. Naturally, it was lighter stuff because it was an acoustic. Then we started listening to Diamanda Galas and John Paul Jones' *Sporting Life* and we said, 'Wait a minute! Rock and roll! Let's rock.' So I got a Fender Shenandoah electric 12-string. I think it's really wild that I'm playing a lot of 12-string electric because when you look back, there's not a lot of bands that did. Zeppelin did, the Byrds, maybe the Beatles. And for me, it just kind of happened that way.

GW: When you were preparing to record this album, did you woodshed for awhile, or did things develop as you went along?

NOVOSELIC: I developed it as we went. I remember coming up with guitar parts but not really being proficient enough to play them correctly. It took time to really develop as a guitar player. I can play the bass and change the channel on the TV at the same time. Guitar playing takes a lot more concentration.

GW: Well, you do have three times the number of strings to worry about.

NOVOSELIC: Exactly.

GW: Where did you meet Yva?

NOVOSELIC: We met at a birthday party on May 16, 1994. It was my birthday, a surprise party at my house...

LAS VEGAS: ...and his wife had hired me to sing.

NOVOSELIC: Yva was singing some Venezuelan folk songs. I thought she was really good, so we got together. I had some riffs and we started working on songs. Yva told me she had some riffs and songs too, and we put them together. And that was the beginning of Sweet 75.

GW: Do you have any thoughts on the Soundgarden breakup, on their legacy and impact on music in the Nineties?

NOVOSELIC: Oh, my God! Those guys had an impact *early*. I remember seeing them in 1985, when Chris [Cornell] played drums and had a Flock of Seagulls haircut. They were doing something different. Everyone else was doing hardcore, but then the Melvins slowed down, Soundgarden slowed down, and that was it. The music was always quality stuff, and they sounded like a band that really had it together. When I heard they broke up, I got all choked up. I really love them and I'm happy for them, because they've never done anything, at least not to my knowledge, where they flew off and got crazy. They've always been very solid, very classy. So I'm sure they thought long and hard before they decided it was time to move on. They left at the top, and it wasn't messy as it often is.

GW: How did you go about recording the album?

NOVOSELIC: A lot of the songs were recorded live. Yva would be in the vocal booth with her bass on and we'd just kind of bash it out.

GW: Do you prefer rehearsing and then recording everything live?

NOVOSELIC: Sometimes. In Nirvana, I always had the kamikaze approach to recording. A lot of the songs on *In Utero* were first takes, just live.

GW: Did anything else carry over from Nirvana?

NOVOSELIC: Sweet 75 is just such a different deal, but there are a few things. The trick is in the interaction between musicians: not only did a person have an instrument that they were playing, but they also had a responsibility to really add that instrument to the song as opposed to just playing. That was what we did in Nirvana: play the song over and over again and try different things out until it came together and you felt it was right. Or you throw the song away, or you save it for later then drag it out again and see if you can make it happen.

I would start by listening to different aspects of the song and try to figure out how to play off the vocal, or play off the bass, or play off the guitar, or just keep the riff steady and keep things anchored down, because you don't want to bum rush the vocal if the vocals are really good. You want to keep your part tied down, and when it's time to bust out, go good and hopefully it will all come out smoothly.

GW: Do you now identify yourself as a guitar player? "Hi, I'm Krist Novoselic, guitar player!"

NOVOSELIC: [*laughing*] No, I just say, "Hi, I'm Krist Novoselic."

LAS VEGAS: [*uncontrolled laughter*] Is that the goal? To say, "I am so and so, *guitar player!*" Oh God!

GW: The *Guitar World* audience would appreciate some kind of proclamation in that direction.

NOVOSELIC: I am a God!

Guitar School, May 1994

Heavy Hitter

Jerry Cantrell takes a look back at some of Alice in Chains' most memorable musical moments.

By Jeff Kitts

ALICE IN CHAINS released its 1990 debut album, *Facelift*, upon a music scene ripe for a hostile grunge takeover. Since then, the Seattle quartet has been caught up in a constant flurry of activity, releasing two EPs, another full-length album and recording various numbers for movie soundtracks, including *Singles* and *Last Action Hero*. Few bands have had that much success in so short a time, but guitarist Jerry Cantrell says he knew there was something special about Alice in Chains the moment he heard their first single.

"We don't write songs with the intention of making them hits," says Cantrell, "but when I first heard 'Man in the Box,' I knew people would dig it."

With *Facelift*, Alice in Chains managed to impress the world with the sheer volume of Cantrell's churning, guitar-driven stomp. But once Alice in Chains became known as one of Seattle's foremost noisemakers, the band decided to show off its sensitive side. They released *Sap*, an all-acoustic EP that features vocal contributions from Soundgarden's Chris Cornell and Heart's Ann Wilson—it was the ideal forum for the band to showcase its versatility as musicians and songwriters.

"Many people didn't even know that we put out *Sap* until way after its release, but that was intentional," says Cantrell. "We were trying to demonstrate that we aren't just a metal band. Even though we are a metal band at times, we like to play all different kinds of music."

Later that year, Alice in Chains plugged in once again to record their second full-length album, *Dirt*. Boasting a vast array of styles, *Dirt* was as challenging and diverse a record as ever came out of the Northwest.

"Even with the success of *Facelift*, there wasn't much pressure when we were working on *Dirt*," says Cantrell. "In fact, it was much easier because we really didn't think about how we wanted the songs to go down. *Dirt* was a lot more free-form. We just kept piling up ideas, and by the time it was done, the album was so massive it totally blew me away."

Recently, Alice in Chains released *Jar of Flies*, a seven-song follow-up to *Sap*. So after four records and a handful of soundtrack contributions, *Guitar School* felt the time was right to catch up with Cantrell, the band's chief composer, to discuss some of the key elements in Alice in Chains' flavorful musical repertoire.

"We Die Young" *Facelift* (Columbia, 1990)

"I remember when I first came up with that riff. It really stuck in my head—it was really violent-sounding. I got the idea for the lyrics from this rough area of Seattle called Seward Park, which has a lot of crack and guns, and is basically controlled by local gangs. I'd see 12-year-olds with beepers every day, and it really amazed me that kids at such a young age could get involved in that world. It scared me to see it, so that's what I wrote the lyrics about."

"Man in the Box" *Facelift*

"That riff was something I had around for quite a while but never did anything with. Layne [*Staley, vocals*] came up with some vocal ideas, and the song eventually came together. Of our early material, the riff that goes through the talkbox is definitely one of my favorites. Layne wrote the lyrics, and I think he was trying to say that people are pretty much like animals who live inside little boxes—that we really only see the bullshit that comes across the tube and in the newspaper."

"It Ain't Like That" *Facelift*

"That riff was actually a mistake I made one day at rehearsal. Sean [*Kinney, drums*] and I were goofing around and I came up with this riff as a joke, but Sean was like, 'Do it again—that was great!' I didn't think anything would come of it, but once we put it together, I realized that it could work. At the time I was just kidding around, playing it with this goofy look on my face."

"Right Turn" *Sap* (Columbia, 1992)

"That song was really fun to do. After I wrote it, I wasn't sure if anything would come of it, but I had this idea of having Chris Cornell [*Soundgarden*] and Mark Arm [*Mudhoney*] help out with the vocals. They came down, sang their respective parts, and it came out really great. When Mark sings that last verse, it's just so heavy. And Cornell just rules—those two guys made that song. Of all our songs, it's definitely one of my favorites. It's got a terrific vibe to it."

"Them Bones" *Dirt* (Columbia, 1992)

"That song actually reminded me of the vibe I got from 'We Die Young.' The riffing has a real intense feel to it. Many people have a hard time dealing with our lyrical content because it's so harsh, like in 'Them Bones.' 'Them Bones' isn't really about death and dying, it's about coming to grips with the time you have left as you get to the end of your life. It's a very sad thing, realizing that you won't last forever. You should try to do as much in the meantime as you can. That's how I live my life."

"Rooster" *Dirt*

"I wrote that song during the *Facelift* days, but never did anything with it. I was over at Chris Cornell's place, and he has this little room about the size of a closet where he does a lot of recording. It's so closed-off that when you're in there, all you can do is focus on your music. I came up with a lot of great song ideas in that room. 'Rooster' was one of those songs, and I've always been very proud of it, both lyrically and musically."

"Sickman" *Dirt*

"Layne asked me one day to write the most screwed-up musical arrangement I could write—he told me to go completely insane and over-the-edge. So I did, and came up with the music to 'Sickman.' It's a really intense song, and it has a lot of different vibes in it. 'Sickman' is one of the best arrangements I've ever done—but it's also the hardest song to play live."

"What the Hell Have I" *Last Action Hero* (Columbia, 1993)

"We didn't write that song for the *Last Action Hero* soundtrack—we just had it around and figured it would be good for the movie. It was basically a song about us dealing with all the confusion that was going on at the time. It was written from me to Layne. We were trying a bunch of different instruments, and I tried a regular sitar, but I didn't know how to play it, so I ended up using a guitar-sitar."

"Whale and Wasp" *Jar of Flies* (Columbia, 1994)

"That's another song that I had lying around for a while. In fact, it's one of my earliest pieces of music—I was probably around 18 or 19 when I wrote it. So when we started writing for *Jar of Flies*, I had to remember how the song went. Mike [*Inez, bass*] talked about putting some strings on the record, and we thought 'Whale and Wasp' would be a good song for that. As for why I called it 'Whale and Wasp,' I did so because that's basically what it sounded like to me—a conversation between a whale and a wasp."

"Rotten Apple" *Jar of Flies*

"That song and 'I Stay Away' were songs that Mike came up with on bass, and then massaged them with my guitar to make them come alive. Besides the stuff on the *Last Action Hero* soundtrack, this was the first material we've written with Mike. He's a really talented guy, and he adds a lot to the band. It was important for us to know that he could do that."

Guitar School, May 1995

Pearl Jams

Guitarist Mike McCready picks the pearls from his rich portfolio of jams.

By Jeff Gilbert

"I'M SO IGNORANT of this technical stuff," says Mike McCready when asked to explain the intricacies of Pearl Jam's hit-making writing process. "I've always done it by ear. Honestly, I'd rather do regular interviews. It's more interesting to talk about whatever...anything other than guitars. I'm not into being a tech-head."

He's just being modest, of course. A guitarist doesn't reach the top of the rock and roll heap without having a solid acquaintance with his instrument and gear. But then again, that's what high-paid roadies are for. McCready, an accomplished musician, is not ashamed about being technically challenged. He prefers to concentrate on the more visceral aspects of rock guitar. Like stealing riffs.

"Everything I know, I stole directly from Ace Frehley, Angus Young and Keith Richards," admits McCready. "That's how you learn. I used to sit for hours and copy every lick on those early AC/DC and Kiss records. From there I went on to Eric Clapton and Stevie Ray Vaughan. After a while, you kind of develop your own style."

Here are a few examples of McCready's best thievery.

"Reach Down" *Temple of the Dog* (A&M, 1990)

"That was my first lead on an album, and I was so excited. I'd been in a studio before, but never to record an album or anything. I did that in one take! I soloed through the whole thing and ended up with the headphones wrapped around my face. I was totally flushed. The guitar work on that track represents one of my proudest moments."

"Hunger Strike" *Temple of the Dog*

"I remember thinking that this was a really beautiful song when I heard it. [Soundgarden's] Chris Cornell showed me the riff. I had a '62 reissue Strat and I wanted to use the fourth-position tone setting—between the bridge and the middle pickups—for the beginning of the song because I like that softer sound. Then I kicked it to the front pickup for the heavier part of the song. This is one of many amazing songs written by Chris."

"Even Flow" *Ten* (Epic, 1991)

"That's me pretending to be Stevie Ray Vaughan, and a feeble attempt at that. Stone [*Gossard, guitarist*] wrote the riff and song; I think it's a D tuning. I just followed him in a regular pattern. I tried to steal everything I know from Stevie Ray Vaughan and put it into that song. A blatant rip-off. A tribute rip-off, if you will."

"Alive" *Ten*

"I copied Ace Frehley's solo from Kiss' 'She,' which was copied from Robby Krieger's solo in the Doors' 'Five to One.' "

"Why Go" *Ten*

"The thing I remember most about this song is how thunderous Jeff Ament's huge 12-string bass was, and me getting to noodle over it. He had just gotten the Hamer Tom Peterson model, and 'Why Go' was the first song he used it on. It sounded like a piano in your face. It was pretty intense."

"Black" *Ten*

"That's more of a Stevie rip-off, with me playing little flowing things. I was way into that trip—I still am, actually, but it was probably more obvious back then. I really thought the song was beautiful. Stone wrote it and he just let me do what I wanted."

"Dirty Frank" "Even Flow" single (Epic, 1992)

"This is a song about our illustrious first bus driver, who we were convinced was a serial killer. [*laughs*] It came out of a jam we had at a soundcheck when we were touring with the Red Hot Chili Peppers. We were influenced by their funky jamming; maybe it's an homage. Eddie [*Vedder, vocals*] came up with the lyrics. We've tried to play it live a couple of times since, but it never works. I've heard it on bootlegs and it's really bad. The recorded version is cool, but we never did it right again."

"Breath" *Singles* soundtrack (Epic, 1992)

"That was a really old song of Stone's from his days in Mother Love Bone. It was just another chance for me to do a lot of leads. The song was kind of cool at the time because it reminded me of performing. For me, it was about playing live."

"Animal" *Vs.* (Epic, 1993)

"I like the lead on that. George Webb, a guy who takes care of all our guitars and amps, was sitting there and I told him I'd do a solo for him. It ended up being the one we used on the record. I did it on a Gibson 335. That's a fun song to play."

"Glorified G" *Vs.*

"I wrote part of that one. I had this Gretsch Country Gentleman and I started jamming on this little thing in D [*sings riff*]; the riff just came out of that. Stone came up with his weird part. There were all these strange, disjointed parts that kind of turned into a song. Stone's doing something weird, Jeff's doing something weird and offbeat, but for some reason it works. I really don't know why."

"Spin the Black Circle" *Vitalogy* (Epic, 1994)

"That's me trying to do Johnny Thunder leads. I actually overdubbed those leads, but when I do it live, that riff is so hectic and frantic, I have to be warmed up or it sounds really shitty."

"Not for You" *Vitalogy*

"Tom Petty sent me this amazing 12-string Rickenbacker, and 'Not for You' was the first time I used it. It was like a Christmas present. One day it just showed up at my door. I called him up and thanked him. But it's a cool song—an Eddie song."

"Tremor Christ" *Vitalogy*

"I wrote part of that one. It's kind of an odd, marching Beatles tune. It's just a strange song. It was written in New Orleans. The groove reconciles itself after you get into it."

"Satan's Bed" *Vitalogy*

"That's another Stone song. The solo is definitely my tribute to Angus Young; I was trying to do my Angus thing. I'm sure Eddie won't like reading that." [*laughs*]

"Catholic Boy" *Basketball Diaries* soundtrack (Island, 1995)

"Jeff and I did that song with Jim Carroll, who wrote the song and the book the movie is based on. Jim came out to Seattle and Chris Friel, a friend of mine [*from McCready's high school band, Shadow*], played drums. Eddie plays guitar, Jim sings, I play guitar, Jeff plays bass—Stone was off doing something else. We cut it at Bad Animals Studio in a day. We got to hang out with Jim Carroll all day. He's so cool."

GUITAR WORLD

PRESENTS

Guitar World Presents is an ongoing series of books filled with extraordinary interviews, feature pieces and instructional material that have made *Guitar World* magazine the world's most popular musicians' magazine. For years, *Guitar World* has brought you the most timely, the most accurate and the most hard-hitting news and views about your favorite players. Now you can have it all in one convenient package: *Guitar World Presents.*

Guitar World Presents Classic Rock
00330370 (304 pages, 6" x 9") $17.95

Guitar World Presents Alternative Rock
00330369 (352 pages, 6" x 9") $17.95

Guitar World Presents Nirvana and the Grunge Revolution
00330368 (240 pages, 6" x 9") $16.95

Guitar World Presents Kiss
00330291 (144 pages, 6" x 9") $14.95

Guitar World Presents Van Halen
00330294 (208 pages, 6" x 9") $14.95

Guitar World Presents Metallica
00330292 (144 pages, 6" x 9") $14.95

Guitar World Presents Stevie Ray Vaughan
00330293 (144 pages, 6" x 9") $14.95

FOR MORE INFORMATION, SEE YOUR LOCAL MUSIC DEALER,
OR WRITE TO:

HAL•LEONARD®
CORPORATION
7777 W. BLUEMOUND RD. P.O. BOX 13819 MILWAUKEE, WI 53213

Prices and availability subject to change without notice.
Some products may not be available outside the U.S.A.